Value & Reference
Guide to Collecting

Living Dead Dolls™

Robin Moore

Schiffer® Publishing Ltd
4880 Lower Valley Road, Atglen, PA 19310 USA

Dedication

In loving memory of my best friend, Desireé, with an Iron Will and a Velvet Heart she died too young and too soon. Can you see your violets are in bloom! Until we meet again, my friend, may you rest in Jesus!

Disclaimer

This book is in no way affiliated with Mezco Toyz™ LLC, LivingDeadDolls.com™ LLC, Bleeding Edge™ Goths, Teddy Scares™ or Krypt Kiddies™

Published by Schiffer Publishing Ltd.
4880 Lower Valley Road
Atglen, PA 19310
Phone: (610) 593-1777; Fax: (610) 593-2002
E-mail: Info@schifferbooks.com

For the largest selection of fine reference books on this and related subjects, please visit our web site at **www.schifferbooks.com**
We are always looking for people to write books on new and related subjects. If you have an idea for a book please contact us at the above address.

This book may be purchased from the publisher.
Include $3.95 for shipping.
Please try your bookstore first.
You may write for a free catalog.

In Europe, Schiffer books are distributed by
Bushwood Books
6 Marksbury Ave.
Kew Gardens
Surrey TW9 4JF England
Phone: 44 (0) 20 8392-8585; Fax: 44 (0) 20 8392-9876
E-mail: info@bushwoodbooks.co.uk
Free postage in the U.K., Europe; air mail at cost.

Library of Congress Cataloging-in-Publication Data

Moore, Robin, 1964 Aug. 18.
Value & reference guide to collecting Living Dead dolls / Robin Moore.
p. cm.
ISBN 0-7643-2293-1 (pbk.)
1. Living Dead dolls—Collectors and collecting—Catalogs. I. Title: Value and reference guide to collecting Living Dead dolls. II. Title.

NK4894.3.L58M66 2005
688.7'221'0973075—dc22

2005010569

Designed by "Sue"
Type set in fontdinerdotcom/Zurich BT

ISBN: 0-7643-2293-1
Printed in China
1 2 3 4

Acknowledgments

With special thanks:

To the Lord Jesus Christ. His saving grace gave me the courage and strength to make this guide a reality.

To my Mom Jenny, for your love, friendship, prayers, believing in me, feeding me, and doing my laundry.

To my wonderful 80-year-old friend, Betty, for ironing my laundry and making me laugh on a daily basis! May God bless you always!

To fellow Living Dead Dolls™ collector and ordained minister Mike Blackwell for your knowledge, prayers, and life-changing words.

To fellow Living Dead Dolls™ collector Stephen Schweckendieck and his "Beez Bloody Dumping Groundz" for taking many of the awesome photos in this book. He has almost every doll in his collection and was kind enough to let me browse his photo album "These Are the Dayz of Our Dollz." I begged, I borrowed, and he came through. A huge Thanks!

To Kirsty Pickup, Frank Mitman, Judy Buttram, Randy and Rodonna Murawski, Mike Richards, Nick Hayes, Ian Pendlebury, Jesse Soberman, and Veda Darby who participated in the making of this book by sharing their collections, stories, and photographs.

To Living Dead Dolls, LLC for taking the time to answer my many daunting questions and for being so creative. Keep up the pure evil!

To Steve Varner, Toni Deaso, and Matthew Coffin at Bleeding Edge™ Goths for supplying photographs and for always being so totally AWESOME!

Robin fabricated and wore this 6-foot long and 4-foot wide coffin costume; she entered it into three Halloween contests and won three first place prizes to win a whopping $5000. This was a literal graveyard on wheels complete with handmade mask, chest & clothing. Electronic rats eating moving bloody squirting guts, rotting skeleton and human legs with every kind of bug imaginable and of course a tombstone.

To Phil Nannay and Joe DiDomenico at Teddy Scares™ for supplying all their photographs and for going above and beyond the call of duty. You guys ROCK!

To Ed and Rita Uhl at Krypt Kiddies™ for sharing their story and photographs. You guys creep me out… uh, I mean your kiddies do!

To Robert C. Whitus and Chris Johnson at drinkwiththelivingdead.com for supplying all their photographs and for the way wicked cool drinking glasses. Keep up the great work!

To Stormie Omartian, "The Power of a Praying Woman," which helped me to believe and be born again in Christ.

To Billy Graham, author of *The Holy Spirit,* which gave me the gift to write this book!

Contents

This Book Belongs To

Introduction 6

Series One 14

Series Two 19

Series Three 22

Series Four 25

Series Five 28
Series Five Black & White Set 31
Series Five Club Mez Chase Set 32
Series Five Blood Spattered Jezebel 33
Mail Away Handmade Sadie 34

Series Six: 666 35

Series Seven: Seven Deadly Sins 38

Exclusives 42

Dead Dollies 58

Ragdolls 59

Porcelain Series 61

Fashion Victims 62

Mini Series 67

Other Items 73

Handmade & Prototype Dolls 80

Blood Spattered Eggzorcist 92

Magazine Advertisements 93

Checklist 95
Bleeding Edge™ Goths 104
Krypt Kiddies™ 109
Teddy Scares™ 111

Introduction

Damien Glonek and Ed Long created Living Dead Dolls™ in 1998. They were handmade and sold at horror conventions like the Monster Bash in Pittsburgh, Pennsylvania, and the Chiller Theatre in Rutherford, New Jersey. It was at the Chiller Theatre horror convention in 2000 that CEO Michael "Mez" Markowitz of Mezco Toyz™ purchased one of these handmade Living Dead Dolls™. A few weeks later Mez contacted the guys to create a partnership that would prove to be an incredible journey for them all.

Mezco Toyz was established in 2000. Through an agreement it was decided that they would take over manufacturing of the dolls that would continue to be based on the exclusive designs of Damien and Ed.

With a huge worldwide fan base, Living Dead Dolls™ has become the hottest collectible since Frankenstein took his bride! Damien and Ed are said to have a simple rule of thumb they follow when creating each doll. They create dolls that are aesthetically appealing or, as some would say, horrifically wonderful. Their concern is not for how much money it may make or even if the collector will like it. In collecting their creepy creations I suggest you should also keep the same thing in mind. Collect what you LOVE! That's the best advice you should take when starting your Living Dead Dolls™ collection.

At the time of this writing the Fashion Victims Series II and a few new products, like the Living Dead Dollies™, Living Dead Ragdolls™ Exclusive Halloween Costumes, have been created and were scheduled for release in 2004. The partnership of Damien, Ed and Mezco Toyz™ has come along way since 2000 when Series I was first released with a set of 5 dolls. They are well on their way to 100+ different items now available, including exclusive twin pack dolls, mini 7 pack dolls, mini 3 pack dolls, International Exclusives from the United Kingdom & Germany, porcelain dolls, party lights, a board game, stationary, and more.

Damien & Ed have also made available via their web site *www.livingdeaddolls.com* other items, including trading cards, T-shirts, and pin back buttons, to name a few. They have autographed many dolls and other items and their signatures are commonly found. You can also find autographed certificates of authenticity included with various handmade dolls and the mini FX exclusive Eggzorcist limited to 3,000 pieces.

If you own an early version handmade or prototype doll and it is autographed or comes with a certificate of authenticity it is probably authentic. If you have one of these dolls with or without an autograph you can email a picture of your doll to Damien and Ed send or take it to them. They'll authenticate your doll and perhaps give you a signed certificate of authenticity. If you are looking to purchase one of these early handmade dolls and the seller doesn't have any authentication, I recommend contacting the creators for more information.

On average the value of an autographed doll having the signatures of Damien Glonek and Ed Long will increase its value about $10 to $20 depending on the rarity of the item. That's actually not too bad considering most autographs of famous movie stars are worth $50 to $80 each. A rarer item like an autographed "Blue Blood Spattered Eggzorcist" limited to only 100 pieces will run you around $700-$800. When these dolls were manufactured, the doll was covered with a black plastic body bag, which needed to be opened to see if the bloody doll was inside. Less than 100 of these were autographed which would make the autographed doll more valuable than the doll without the autograph, which would be valued at the lesser value of $500-$600. Yes, in this particular instance Damien and Ed's signatures would be valued at right around $100-$200. WOW! The actual autographs were also signed to include the words "Real Bloody" with the word REAL being underlined several times. This was done so you would know it was an authentic doll, thus "REAL" and "BLOODY." I have also found dolls to include Damien, Ed, and Mez signatures. The Mez signature often times includes the year.

Fake Living Dead Dolls™ do exist and you must be very careful when purchasing the more expensive dolls. With the values of the early handmade and rare dolls climbing as rapidly as they are you'll always have someone out there trying to deceive you to make a quick buck. Here is a great tip for you and one you should stick by when purchasing the more expensive dolls. Do your research, ask lots of questions and if possible ask Damien or Ed at *www.livingdeaddolls.com* for help!

An edition of only 30 Series One Blood Spattered version of the Eggzorcist was made in 2000. The dolls were used as a promotional item to take to the Chiller Theatre Convention when the dolls were first released. Damien and Ed sold 24 of them; I saw one sell at an online auction in April 2003 for $1825. Currently an authentic blood spattered Eggzorcist doll is valued at around $2,000-$2,500.

Within one month after the authentic bloody doll sold online for $1825, a fake doll surfaced from an online seller asking a mere $800. It would appear through research that the thief seeks out the highest selling toys or other items they can find at online auctions and tries to duplicate them in some manner. To accomplish this feat a thief would have to open a regular Series One Eggzorcist doll, paint some blood on it & reseal the package. The dolls are identical with the exception of the blood spatter, therefore making the doll an easy target for fraudulent duplication.

The fraudulent seller then offers a fake doll to online auction buyers who missed the previous auction, while interest is still peaked from the sale of the real doll. They will usually contact the next highest bidder and work down the list until they find someone who is not armed with knowledge about the doll. That the fake doll was NOT autographed and had an asking price of only $800 should have been red flags to the purchaser! Several other authentic dolls have sold at online auctions swapping hands among legitimate collectors a few times.

If you plan on purchasing any of the rare dolls I recommend keeping track of any sales you might find. Use EXTREME CAUTION before purchasing this doll or any other one-of-a-kind or handmade dolls! Contact Damien or Ed for more information.

Fraudulent Sellers are out there waiting to trick someone who is not armed with the proper information.

If it sounds too good to be true it usually is. A good rule of thumb to follow is most people will not offer items for less then their real value, especially if the same item just sold at an online auction. I have found many fake dolls while doing research for this book. Some folks are pretty crafty and with computer-age graphics can easily duplicate identical packaging. Always use caution when buying from unknown online auctions or sellers. The most fraud is committed there. The best way to protect yourself is to ask lots of questions, study this book and gain as much knowledge as you can. I have attempted to make it as accurate as I can to help you. You'll save yourself some heartache, time and money by doing so. And above all you won't be lining the pockets of thieves.

The Best Advice is to always purchase your more expensive dolls from reputable online or local dealers in your area. There are many reputable dealers online all over the world. I recommend doing extensive research before shelling out $1,000 for a rare doll. You can also ask Damien and Ed to authenticate a doll for you. They are the best source because they made the dolls by hand. They are very approachable and make many appearances at local horror conventions and toy shows like the San Diego Comic-Con where they answer questions and autograph dolls. You can also reach them via email at *info@livingdeaddolls.com*. Keep in mind they're busy guys and will get back to you when they can.

Exclusives are made for toy distribution companies or "BIG RETAILERS." What this means is that Mezco Toyz™ will make a doll, dolls, or other items solely for a particular distributor or retailer to be sold by that company exclusively.

Some of the distributors and retailers include Diamond Comics, Marz Distribution, Spencer Gifts, Tower Records, and Hot Topic. You can also find these items from "small retailers" online or locally in your area. The small retail outlets will also carry many of the older exclusive items that have been long sold out.

These dolls are Sooooo HOT that the big retailers buy up a major portion of the manufacturer's or distributor's stock. They usually purchase more than they can handle or so it would seem.

Example: have you ever walked into a Tower Records or Spencer Gifts and found a large quantity of older items just sitting there on the shelf collecting dust? Me too. In fact I search them out! When this happens you usually find big discounts.

Finding sales on the exclusive items is quite easy because sales & marketing for the big retailers may be limited. This is where you as a collector come into play, and sometimes you can find huge sales with discounts up to 75% off. Big retailers are limited in their sales outlets. They may not ship internationally, don't have online stores, or their local brick and mortar stores are in areas that don't have a following or need for the items. The bottom line is when the big retailer has exhausted every avenue of selling a particular item or their sales are slow they sell at discounted prices.

All you need is patience, a willingness to search for the items, and, of course, a small amount of cash. You can find these sales online at small retailers, Tower Records, or at your local Spencer Gifts to name a few. It may take some diligent hunting , but you can find sale items and use them to complete your collection. There will always be a sale somewhere waiting for you because not everyone knows how to sell a hot product like the Living Dead Dolls™.

Online Auctions are great sources for rare and hard to find dolls and other items, and sometimes you can buy them for as little as half of the real value of the items. You must use "CAUTION" when purchasing from online auctions. Ask questions, lots of questions. Don't rely on the descriptions to be accurate unless you know you are dealing with a well-known, reputable dealer.

Determining the real condition is a common problem when purchasing Living Dead Dolls™ from online auctions. Here's a true story about a Died & Doom Tower Records Exclusive Set that was purchased from an online auction. The seller had a 99.7% positive 400+ feedback rating. It was everything you should look for in an auction including the auction description which clearly stated this exactly: *"Up for auction is a Tower Exclusive Living Dead Doll Died & Doom by Mezco. These dolls have never been opened and are sealed in original plastic, mint and untouched."*

When I received this set of dolls in the mail the original shrink-wrap had a visually detracting hole where a price sticker was removed right on the front of the package. Not on the back or the side but right on the front where obviously the dolls are to be displayed. Needless to say I was disappointed and contacted the seller via email to state my dissatisfaction? After all the description in the auction stated these dolls were *"sealed in original plastic, mint and untouched"* The seller promptly wrote me back to tell me I should have asked questions first and also that he'd owned the dolls for a couple of years, he bought them from an online auction that way and he didn't have a problem with the hole, so why should I?

It wasn't the first time this sort of thing happened to me; I had five instances like this all happen in that same week. Since that day I have lessened the chance by asking five questions every single

time I am interested in
purchasing Living Dead Dolls™
from an online auction. I recommend
you ask them too.

5 Questions to Ask:

1) Is this item sealed in original factory shrink-wrap?
2) Are there any tears in the shrink-wrap?
3) Are there any dents in the box?
4) Are there any stickers or sticker residue on the box?
5) Do you combine shipping for multiple purchases?

You may find more questions you need to ask. Ask as many as you can think of to help in your purchasing decision. I always ask the last question because I've found many times when a seller refuses to combine shipping they are usually gouging or not telling the truth about the items they are selling. You cannot in most cases recover the shipping fees a seller may charge. This has been my experience, anyway, and I have been buying at online auctions for over 5 years.

A Gothic Revival, of sorts, is underway. Take old black & white films like "Nosferatu" from the 1920s, a horror movie like "The Omen" from the 1970s, add a little mystery, mix it with some blood, and you have the hottest NEW collectible of the 21st Century. The question is "do Living Dead Dolls™ have staying power?" Will they be collected 20, 50 or even 100 years from now? Only time will tell. Personally I'd place my bets with Living Dead Dolls™ for a great return on my investment...right now!

So peer into your coffins but open them not, for the value of this unopened collection has the potential to triple or quadruple if stored & taken care of properly. If you would have purchased the Series One Posey released in 2000 for its original selling price of $20-$30, your profit on the open market today would be a *minimum* of $180. I don't know of any bank in the world that would give you that kind of return on a $20 bill.

My Value Guide is in no way affiliated with Mezco Toyz™, Living Dead Dolls™, Damien Glonek or Ed Long. The values in this book are based on retail and secondary market values taken over the last two years from online auctions, stores, and our online collectible retail toy store, *www.WackyStacker.com*. This value and reference guide is to help you identify and determine an approximate value for your dolls and other items.

The prices in this guide are not carved in stone, but rather serve as a starting point to inform and guide you. I personally have compiled the following information over the last two years to obtain average selling prices. You may find some collectible shops selling the same items for more than the prices listed here and in some cases for much less. An item is only worth what someone is willing to pay. You won't find any record high pricing hype here. Estimates have been given for the one-of-a-kind handmade dolls. The estimates given are what we might offer the item for sale in our online store.

Over the past two years I have tested secondary market values to determine the top dollar that someone was willing to pay. I have also tested what kind of prices it would take to make an item fly off the shelf and at what point no one is willing to buy. We have attempted to carry every single Living Dead Dolls™ item made by Mezco Toyz™, and more, so I could write this book. I wanted it to be as accurate as possible. The values and information included here are accurate at the time of printing which brings me to supply and demand.

Supply and demand will dictate the value of your collection and the prices you might pay for your individual Living Dead Dolls™. One of the most basic concepts of collecting anything is supply and demand.

Supply is how much of something is available. For example, if you have nine Living Dead Dolls™, then your supply is nine. Demand is how much of something collectors want. For example, if six collectors want Living Dead Dolls™, then we can say that the demand is six. Okay, so we have supply, which is how much of something you have, and demand, which is how much of something collectors want. Put the two together, and you have supply and demand.

Now, how do you show the relationship between the two? One way is to use the price of something. Generally speaking, the price of something will go up if the demand goes up. Why? Because the seller thinks they can get more money for whatever they are selling.

If more collectors want something, they will be willing to pay more for it. A good example is when an exclusive Living Dead Doll is released. Everybody wants one, and they are willing to pay more than they normally would to get it. The demand goes up because more collectors want them. The price also goes up because the seller knows they can get more money for the exclusive because it is in demand.

In the same way, the price will go down when the demand goes down. When the next exclusive Living Dead Doll is released, everyone wants the new one. The old one doesn't sell as well anymore. The seller still wants to sell the not-so-new doll, since they have a lot still in stock. So, the price goes down. Why? The seller hopes that collectors will be willing to buy the not so new doll at a lower price.

However when we are dealing with a "HOT" item like Living Dead Dolls™ we do eventually reach a point where the older the dolls become, the more valuable they are. Why? Collectors buy the dolls when they were first released and many opened the packages to peek inside. When this happens the supply for sealed dolls goes down, demand increases, which in turn increases the value. A collector who collects for investment does not open the packages.

Let's say you have a one of a kind handmade prototype Living Dead Doll. The supply is 1; the demand is for example 100 collectors so he who has the most money wins. Get It?!

What does all this mean anyway? It means that you can track the supply and demand of your Living Dead Dolls™ collection by tracking the price. If a particular doll has a high price, you can usually conclude that the demand for that doll is high. (This is not always the case; it is usually the case.) In the same way, if a doll has a low price, you can usually conclude that the demand for that doll is low. Studying the two of them and comparing their prices over time can give you a good idea of which dolls are in demand and which are not.

When collecting anything, keep in mind that supplies and values change quickly, and new sales dictate new values. Rarities are discovered, fakes appear, and new items are manufactured.

This book is easy to read and easy to use. No thrills and no frills, just good old-fashioned information about your collection. You may find these abbreviations:

MSC = Mint Sealed Coffin
MOC = Mint Opened Coffin
MIB = Mint in Box
MIP = Mint in Package
MOB = Mint Opened Box
MOP = Mint Opened Package

Body parts are plastic vinyl. When I purchased my first set of dolls the white Sinister Minister 2-pack set I thought they were made of porcelain because of the white bodies. It wasn't until a few months later that I discovered they weren't porcelain at all but rather a fine looking white plastic.

The bodies have some articulation and can be posed at the shoulders, thighs & necks. They've taken a standard 10" tall plastic doll body and turned it in to the most way wicked cool doll I've ever seen! A new doll body with ball joints is scheduled for release with Series 9. The new doll bodies will have a greater range of motion or articulation then their predecessor. The backs of the dolls are all stamped as seen below with the Living Dead Dolls™, Mezco Toyz™ LLC., YEAR and Made in China. Each doll is stamped with different years starting in 2001.

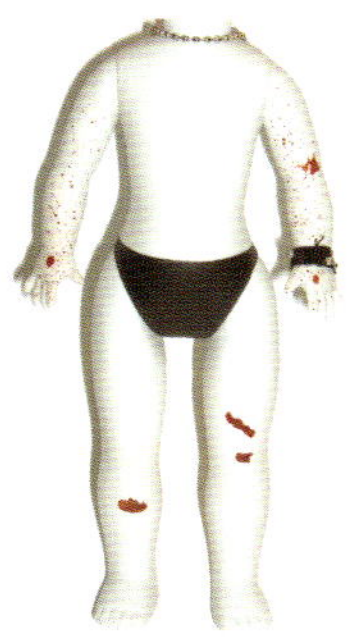

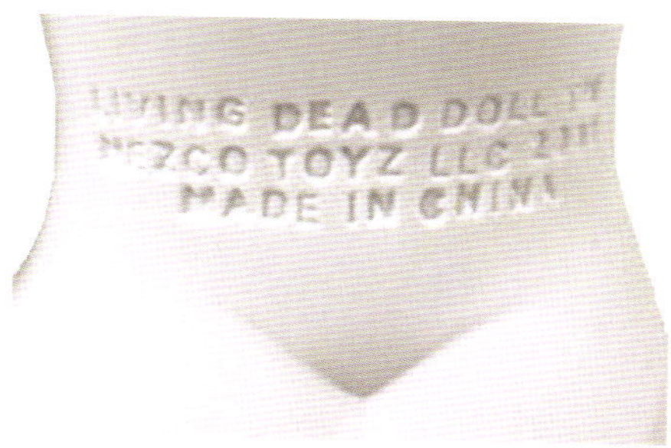

What makes Living Dead Dolls™ so unique is their killer accessories, creepy eyes & bloody or 3-D effects used on many of the dolls. You get the feeling they are really wounded.

Most of the 10" dolls
come with death certificates. I
say most because a few have hand
written style notes or poems. Most of the
certificates look like the one seen below and
Series 5 came with Los Angeles Coroner's Reports
with ID photos.

Death Certificate

I hereby certify that on the Ninth day of August, 1969, at 12:01 A.M.,

Died & Doom

has been pronounced legally deceased.

No wedding night bliss for this bride and groom.
That murdered each other on their honeymoon.
They hated one another right from the start.
But not even death could keep them apart.

Damien Glonek & Ed Long — Morticians
8-9-69 — Date

Living Dead Dolls

Mezco

Other interesting certificates included with some of the dolls were a contract with Series Two Lou Sapphire, a note to the police department with Jack the Ripper, and two items, a Death Certificate plus a Postmortem Marriage License, with Died & Doom.

Postmortem Marriage License

&

I hereby certify that on the Ninth day of August, 1969, at 12:02 A.M.,

As punishment for the sins of their crime,
they shall remain together till the end of time.
It is hereby pronounced that this bride and groom
be wed into blasphemy as

Died & Doom

Witnesses: Sadie
Witnesses: Sin

Signed by: Sinister Minister
Date: 8-9-69

Living Dead Dolls

Mezco

Other unique features included are attached tails, horns, and rooted hair, to name only a few.

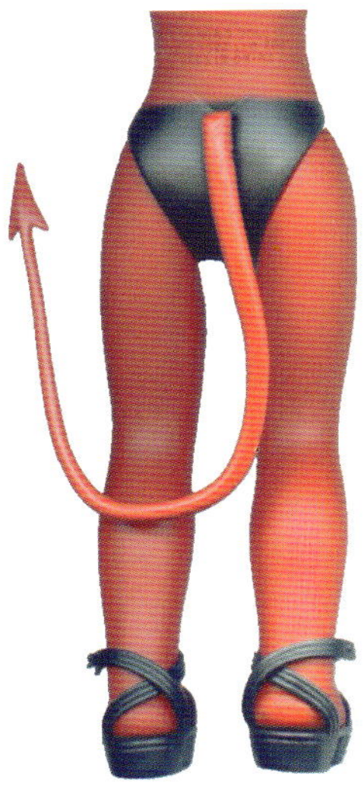

I am searching for interesting stories and photographs. If you would like to have your rare, handmade or prototype dolls, ink drawings, fakes, or any other items of interest for our second issue please visit us at *www.Wackystacker.com* or write us at *LilGothicShop@wackystacker.com*.

Series 1

Series 1 was released as a five doll set in March 2001, with an estimated production run of 4,000 sets. Many of the Living Dead Dolls™ produced are fashioned after movie characters, actual murder victims, or the murderers themselves. Damien is patterned after the 1970s "Demon Child" character from the movie "The Omen," while "Sadie" appears to be patterned after an actual killer "Susan Atkins" from the well-known "Helter Skelter" or "Tate-Bianca" murders.Damien came with a death certificate, small slingshot, and three books. Each doll also comes with a distinctive poem and unique sketch on the labels.

Series 1: Damien

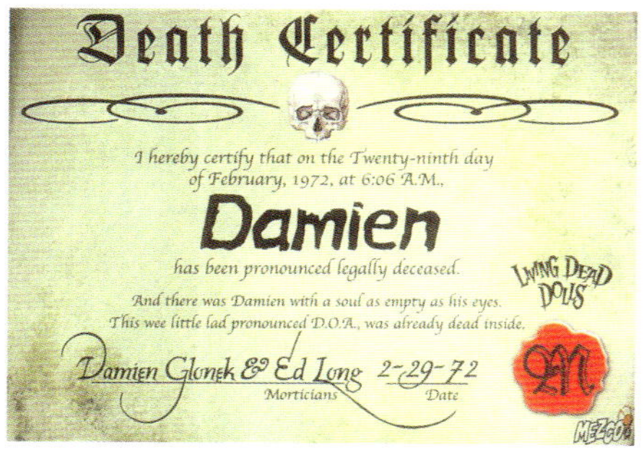

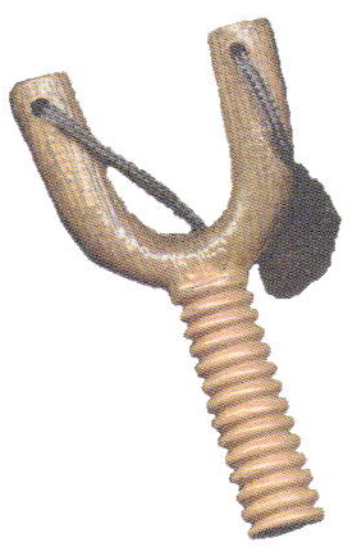

Damien MSC: $90-$120 ~ MOC: $40-$60

Eggzorcist came with an Easter basket, spotted roach, and death certificate

Photos courtesy of Stephen Schweckendieck and www.wackystacker.com

Death Certificate

I hereby certify that on the Fifteenth day of July, 1967, at 3:04 P.M.,

Eggzorcist

has been pronounced legally deceased.

A drawstring used to fasten ears of a rabbit, put this little bunny in a Kiddie Casket.

Damien Glonek & Ed Long — Morticians

7-15-67 — Date

Living Dead Dolls

MEZCO

MSC: \$180-\$240 ~ MOC: \$100-\$120

Series 1: Posey

Posey came with a small rose and a death certificate

Photos courtesy of Stephen Schweckendieck
and www.wackystacker.com

Death Certificate

I hereby certify that on the Eighth day
of August, 1970, at 4:01 A.M.,

Posey

has been pronounced legally deceased.

Poor little Posie was buried alive. Some things
won't stay dead, even after they've died.

Damien Glonek & Ed Long — Morticians

8-8-70 — Date

LIVING DEAD DOLLS

MEZCO

MSC: $200-$240 ~ MOC: $100-$140

Series 1: Sadie

Photos courtesy of Stephen Schweckendieck and www.wackystacker.com

Sadie came with a coffin purse, bloody knife, flower bouquet, and a death certificate

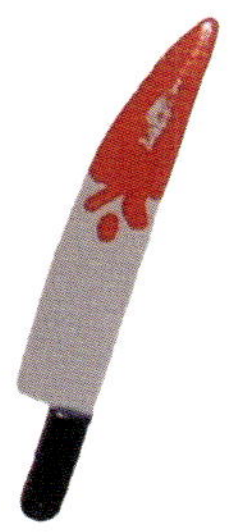

Death Certificate

I hereby certify that on the Twenty-sixth day of April, 1969, at 3:33 A.M.,

Sadie

has been pronounced legally deceased.

No one cared how she turned up dead. So Sadie chose to rise instead. Being easily forgotten wouldn't be fair, Death was something this child had to share.

Damien Glonek & Ed Long — Morticians

4-26-69 — Date

Living Dead Dolls

MEZCO

MSC: $100-$120 ~ MOC: $60-$70

Photos courtesy of Stephen Schweckendieck and www.wackystacker.com

Sin came with a three-pronged pitchfork and death certificate

Death Certificate

I hereby certify that on the Sixth day of June, 1966, at 3:33 P.M.,

Sin

has been pronounced legally deceased.

Sweet little Sin consumed by flames at seven.
Better to forever serve in hell,
than grow up and play in heaven.

Damien Glonek & Ed Long — Morticians
6-6-66 — Date

Living Dead Dolls
Mezco

MSC: $100-$120 ~ MOC: $60-80

Series 2

Series 2 was released as a five doll set in October 2001 with an estimated production run of 7,500 sets. Included in this set is "Deadbra Ann," which appears to be patterned after the 1970s "Prom Queen" character from the movie "Carrie," while "Lizzie Borden" is based on the infamous accused killer with the well-known poem, "Lizzie Borden took an axe and gave her mother 40 whacks, and when she saw what she had done, she gave her father 41."

Series 2: Kitty

Death Certificate

I hereby certify that on the Twenty Eighth day of October, 1997, at 4:50 P.M.,

Kitty

has been pronounced legally deceased.

E - is for everything hateful inside
V - is for vengeance and unholy pride
I - is for infidels shall be eaten by ghouls
L - is for lustfully disposing of fools.

Damien Glonek & Ed Long — Morticians
10-28-97 — Date

Photos courtesy of Stephen Schweckendieck and www.wackystacker.com

Kitty came with a death certificate, bullhorn, and pompoms. Each doll also came with real cloth clothes and rooted hair.

Kitty MSC: $100-$120 ~ MOC: $60-$80

Series 2: Lou Sapphire

Photos courtesy of Stephen Schweckendieck and www.wackystacker.com

Lou Sapphire came with a skull head cane, contract, and death certificate

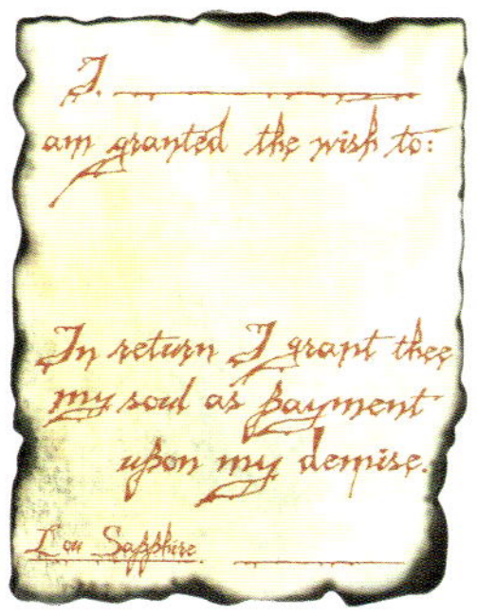

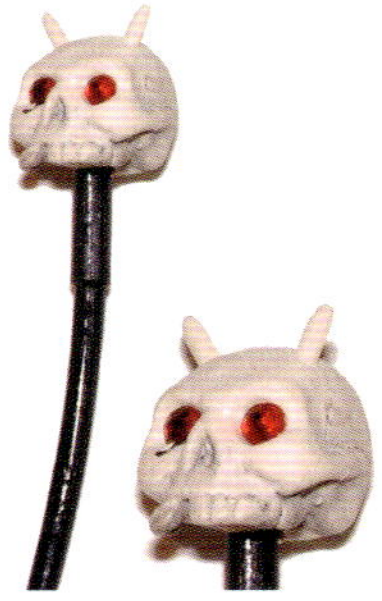

Death Certificate

I hereby certify that on the Thirtieth day of April, 1966, at 12:01 A.M.,

Lou Sapphire

has been pronounced legally deceased.

He died by flame but has returned
His clothes quite cool and souls will burn.

Damien Glonek & Ed Long — Morticians
4-30-66 — Date

Living Dead Dolls

MSC: $80-$90 ~ MOC: $40-$60

Series 2: Lizzie Borden

Photos courtesy of Stephen Schweckendieck and www.wackystacker.com

Lizzie came with a bloody axe and a death certificate

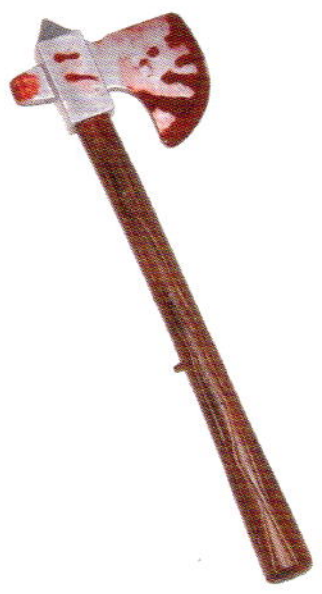

Death Certificate

I hereby certify that on the First day of June, 1927, at 3:13 A.M.,

Lizzie Borden

has been pronounced legally deceased.

Lizzie Borden took an axe
and gave her mother forty whacks.
And when she saw what she had done,
she gave her father forty-one.

Damien Glonek & Ed Long — Morticians
6-1-27 — Date

Living Dead Dolls

MSC: $100-$120 ~ MOC: $60-$70

Series 2: Deadbra Ann

Photos courtesy of Stephen Schweckendieck and www.wackystacker.com

Deadbra Ann came with a flower bouquet, tiara, and death certificate

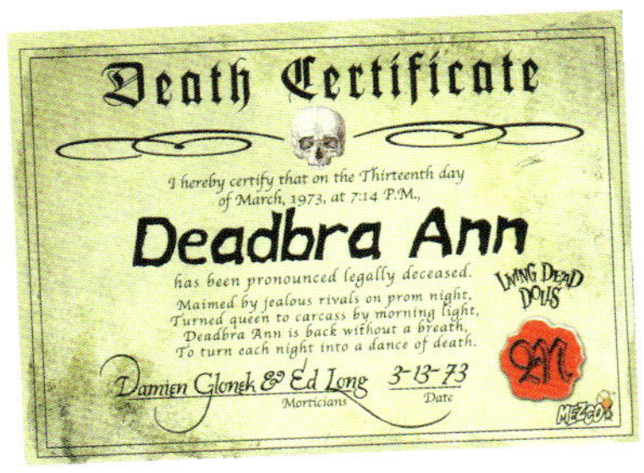
Death Certificate

I hereby certify that on the Thirteenth day of March, 1973, at 7:14 P.M.,

Deadbra Ann

has been pronounced legally deceased.

Maimed by jealous rivals on prom night,
Turned queen to carcass by morning light,
Deadbra Ann is back without a breath,
To turn each night into a dance of death.

Damien Glonek & Ed Long — Morticians
3-13-73 — Date

MSC: $80-$90 ~ MOC: $40-$50

Series 2: School Time Sadie

School Time Sadie came with a schoolbag, bloody hatchet, schoolbook, and note from school

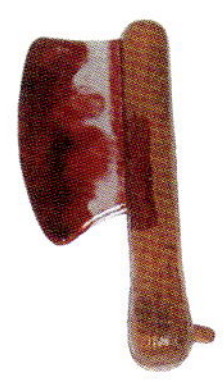

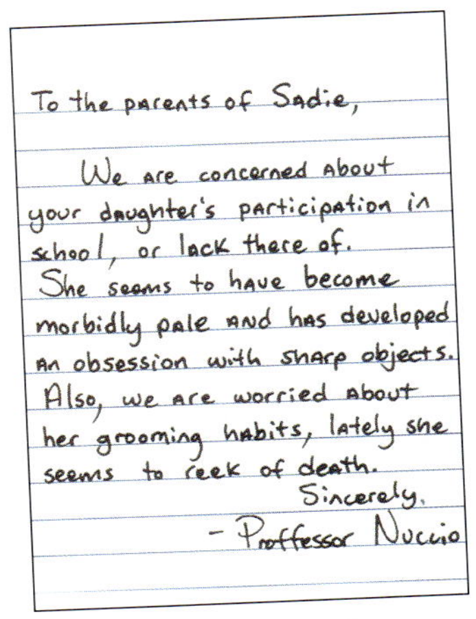
To the parents of Sadie,

We are concerned about your daughter's participation in school, or lack there of. She seems to have become morbidly pale and has developed an obsession with sharp objects. Also, we are worried about her grooming habits, lately she seems to reek of death.

Sincerely,
– Proffessor Nuccio

Photos courtesy of www.wackystacker.com

MSC: $90-$110 ~ MOC: $40-70

Series 3

Series 3 was released as a five doll set in March 2002 with an estimated production run of 8,000 sets. Many of the Living Dead Dolls™ share their death dates with the birth dates of famous people. "Sheena," for example, shares hers with singer "Joey Ramone." Also included in this set is "Schitzo" based on the infamous serial killer "John Wayne Gacy," known as "The Killer Clown."

Series 3: Sheena

Death Certificate

I hereby certify that on the Fifteenth day of April, 2001 at 2:40 P.M.,

Sheena

has been pronounced legally deceased.

Diving off the stage
Sheena landed on her head
She has risen from the grave
Because PUNKS NOT DEAD

Damien Glonek & Ed Long — Morticians
4-15-2001 — Date

Living Dead Dolls

25

Photos courtesy of Stephen Schweckendieck and www.wackystacker.com

Sheena came with a death certificate and bloody spiked baseball bat.

Photos courtesy of Stephen Schweckendieck and www.wackystacker.com

Sheena MSC: $70-$80 ~ MOC: $40-$50

Series 3: Schitzo

Photos courtesy of Stephen Schweckendieck and www.wackystacker.com

Schitzo came with a balloon bouquet and death certificate

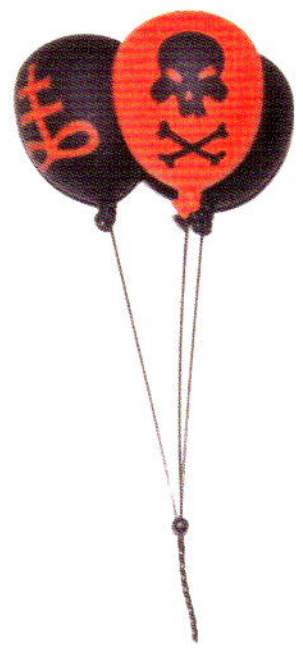

Death Certificate

I hereby certify that on the Thirteenth day of November, 1923, at 12:01 A.M.,

Schitzo

has been pronounced legally deceased.

On the midway of Hell
Schitzo died of laughter
Now he turns each show
Into a bloody disaster

Damien Glonek & Ed Long — Morticians

11-13-1923 — Date

Living Dead Dolls

23

MSC: $40-$50 ~ MOC: $30-$40

Series 3: Lottie

Photos courtesy of Stephen Schweckendieck and www.wackystacker.com

Lottie came with a lace umbrella and death certificate

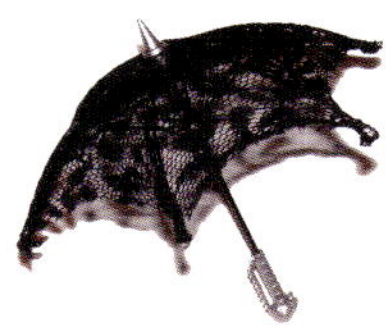

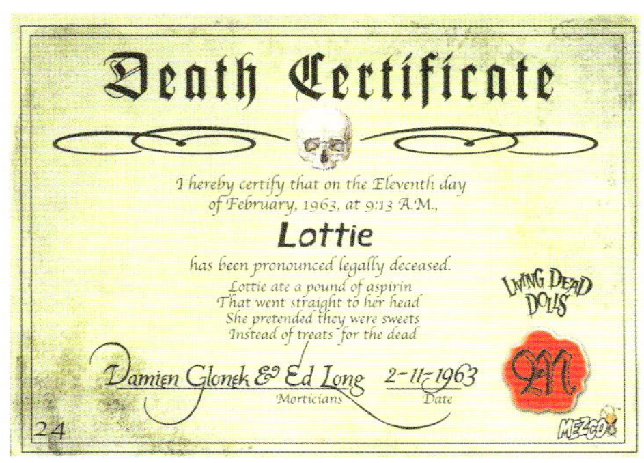
Death Certificate

I hereby certify that on the Eleventh day of February, 1963, at 9:13 A.M.,

Lottie

has been pronounced legally deceased.

Lottie ate a pound of aspirin
That went straight to her head
She pretended they were sweets
Instead of treats for the dead

Damien Glonek & Ed Long — Morticians

2-11-1963 — Date

Living Dead Dolls

24

MSC: $60-$70 ~ MOC: $30-$40

Series 3: Bride of Valentine

Bride of Valentine came with her bloody heart and a death certificate

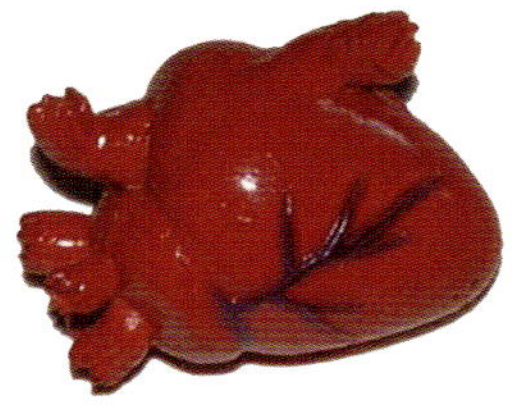

Photos courtesy of Stephen Schweckendieck and www.wackystacker.com

Death Certificate

I hereby certify that on the Fourteenth day
of February, 1929, at 10:30 A.M.,
Bride of Valentine
has been pronounced legally deceased.
This cold unloved bride
Was stitched together with spare parts
The only thing they left out of her
Was a warm still beating heart

Damien Glonek & Ed Long — Morticians
2-14-1929 — Date

Living Dead Dolls

21

Mezco

MSC: $50-$60 ~ MOC: $30-$40

Series 3: Lilith

Photos courtesy of Stephen Schweckendieck and www.wackystacker.com

Lilith came with a bloody vampire stake and a death certificate

Death Certificate

I hereby certify that on the Twenty Seventh day
of December, 1476, at 3:34 P.M.,
Lilith
has been pronounced legally deceased.
Lilith loved all things Goth
Which forced her way into eternal sloth
Now she's damned to wake each night
To feast on blood till morning light

Damien Glonek & Ed Long — Morticians
12-27-1476 — Date

Living Dead Dolls

22

Mezco

MSC: $50-$60 ~ MOC: $30-$40

Series 4

Series 4 was released as a five-doll set in September 2002 with an estimated production run of 9,000 sets. Included in this set is "Sybil" which appears to be patterned after the 1970s "Multiple Personality" character from the movie of the same name. Note each series comes with one boy doll only; this set included the first ethnic boy doll, "Macumba," and the first winged doll, "Inferno."

Series 4: Inferno

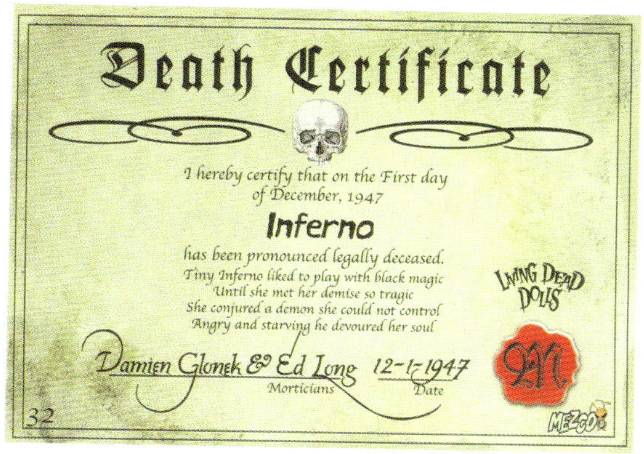
Death Certificate

I hereby certify that on the First day of December, 1947

Inferno

has been pronounced legally deceased.
Tiny Inferno liked to play with black magic
Until she met her demise so tragic
She conjured a demon she could not control
Angry and starving he devoured her soul

Damien Glonek & Ed Long — Morticians
12-1-1947 — Date

Living Dead Dolls
32
Mezco

Photos courtesy of Stephen Schweckendieck and www.wackystacker.com

Inferno came with expandable and retractable wings and a death certificate.

Inferno MSC: $70-$90 ~ MOC: $40-$60

Series4: Macumba

Photos courtesy of Stephen Schweckendieck and www.wackystacker.com

Macumba came with a voodoo doll, skull hat, bone necklace, and a death certificate

Death Certificate

I hereby certify that on the Fifteenth day of June, 1881

Macumba

has been pronounced legally deceased.
Placed under a voodoo curse
It was an evil spell he could not reverse
A soul trapped behind lifeless eyes
All things alive are now despised

Damien Glonek & Ed Long — Morticians
06-15-1881 — Date

Living Dead Dolls
Mezco
34

MSC: $30-$40 ~ MOC: $10-$20

Series 4: Sybil

Photos courtesy of Stephen Schweckendieck and www.wackystacker.com

Sybil came with a straightjacket and a death certificate

Death Certificate

I hereby certify that on the Twenty-First day of December, 1978, at 7:41 A.M.,

Sybil

has been pronounced legally deceased.
Locked away forever insane
The doctors came and removed her brain
She died on the table by morning light
Now in search of a mind she wanders the night

Damien Glonek & Ed Long — Morticians
12-21-1978 — Date

Living Dead Dolls
Mezco
31

MSC: $60-$70 ~ MOC: $40-$50

Series 4: Lulu

Lulu came with a pair of roller skates and a death certificate

Photos courtesy of Stephen Schweckendieck and www.wackystacker.com

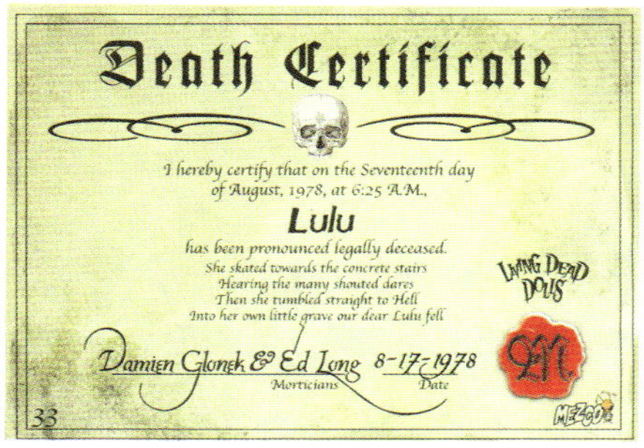
Death Certificate

I hereby certify that on the Seventeenth day of August, 1978, at 6:25 A.M.,

Lulu

has been pronounced legally deceased.

She skated towards the concrete stairs
Hearing the many shouted dares
Then she tumbled straight to Hell
Into her own little grave our dear Lulu fell

Damien Glonek & Ed Long — Morticians
8-17-1978 — Date

LIVING DEAD DOLLS

33

MEZCO

MSC: $80-$100 ~ MOC: $50-$60

Series 4: Ms. Eerie

Ms. Eerie came with a funeral spray of black roses and a death certificate

Photos courtesy of Stephen Schweckendieck and www.wackystacker.com

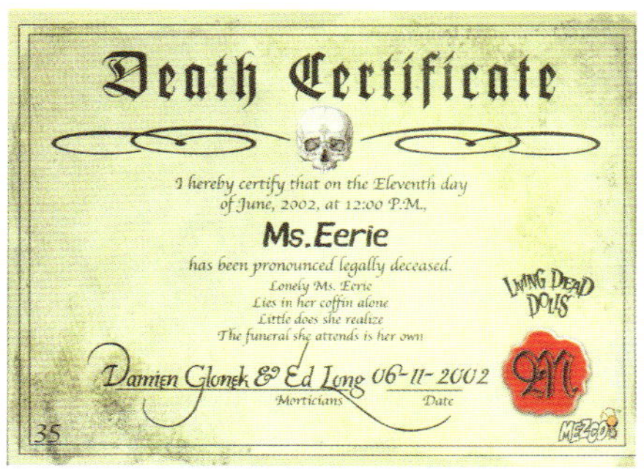
Death Certificate

I hereby certify that on the Eleventh day of June, 2002, at 12:00 P.M.,

Ms.Eerie

has been pronounced legally deceased.

Lonely Ms. Eerie
Lies in her coffin alone
Little does she realize
The funeral she attends is her own

Damien Glonek & Ed Long — Morticians
06-11-2002 — Date

LIVING DEAD DOLLS

35

MEZCO

MSC: $40-$50 ~ MOC: $20-$30

Series 5

Series 5 was released in three different versions of five doll sets in March 2003, with an estimated production run of 10,000 sets. Included in this set is "Dahlia," nicknamed "The Black Dahlia" and based on an unsolved murder in 1947. This was also the first time Los Angeles Coroner's Reports with photo ID's were used in place of the original death certificates. No killer accessories were included with Series 5, which has made them less desirable to collectors.

Series 5: Hollywood

Hollywood came with a real feather boa and a Coroner's Report from the California State Medical Examiner.

Photos courtesy of Stephen Schweckendieck and www.wackystacker.com

Hollywood MSC: $30-$40 ~ MOC: $15-$20

Series 5: Dahlia

Photos courtesy of www.wackystacker.com

Dahlia came with a pearl necklace and a death certificate

MSC: \$25-\$30 ~ MOC: \$10-\$20

Series 5: Jezebel

Photos courtesy of www.wackystacker.com

Jezebel came with a sad heart and a death certificate

MSC: \$25-\$35 ~ MOC: \$10-\$15

Series 5: Siren

Siren came with a black & purple cloak and a death certificate

Photos courtesy of
www.wackystacker.com

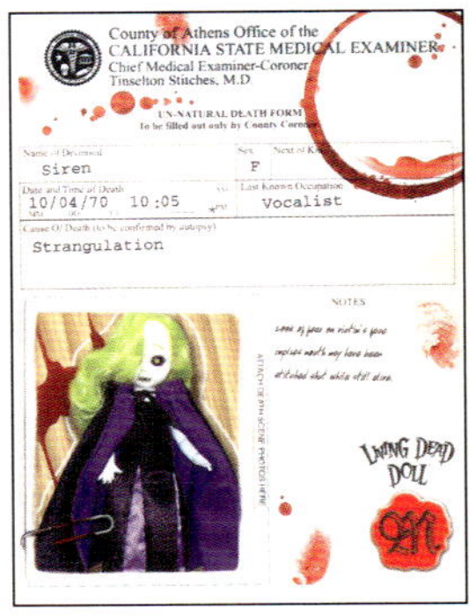

MSC: $30-$35 ~ MOC: $15-$20

Series 5: Vincent

Vincent Vaude came with overalls, bow tie, and a death certificate

Photos courtesy of
www.wackystacker.com

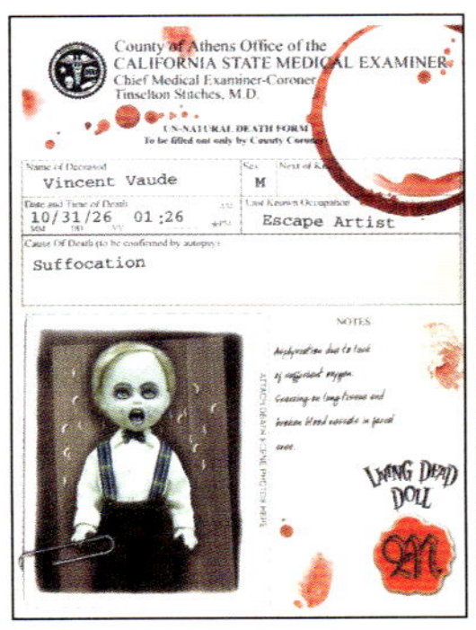

MSC: $15-$20 ~ MOC: $5-$10

Series 5: Black & White Mystery Set

The next set of Series 5 dolls, seen above, was a black & white or mystery "chase" set. One black & white doll was made for every five colored dolls. These could be purchased separately or, sometimes, sellers included them with a set of five colored dolls. The chase dolls were limited to 2,000 pieces of each doll and the coffins sealed with a solid black lid. To reveal which doll was inside, the coffins had to be opened. Concealed among the sealed coffins were five one-of-a-kind black & white blood-spattered dolls.

Valerie & Carlo Trinidad were gracious enough to share this next story with us. They purchased a complete set of sealed mystery chase dolls from a company called Darkside Displays. Each doll came with an X-Ray on a CD with an AVI file showing a full frontal and full profile scan of the doll inside the sealed coffin. Also included were "Certificates of X-Ray" and each coffin was marked on the bottom to show which doll is inside.

I have seen singles like this floating around but never the complete set. The value given below is an estimate of what we might sell the set for in our online store.

Photos courtesy of Valarie & Carlo Trinidad and www.wackystacker.com

Series Five Black & White Mystery MSC: $60-$70 ea MOC: $70-$90 ea Series Five Black & White Mystery Sealed 5 Coffins w/ X-rays & Certificates: $500-$700 set

Series 5: Club Mez Black & White Set

The final set of Series 5 were black & white dolls sold as a Club Mez Exclusive and limited to 666 sets. Purchasing this set was the only way to acquire the black & white dolls with sealed coffins and clear lids, and you had to be a member of the club. The original selling price was $120 for the complete set of five dolls. Opening the packages of this set would destroy the value. Once opened there is no way to tell the difference between the dolls of the Club Mez set and the Mystery Set seen above. The clear lids are the only difference and those come on most every doll made. Never remove the original shrink-wrap from these dolls.

Photos courtesy of www.wackystacker.com

Series Five Club Mez Exclusive B/W Limited to 666 pieces MSC: $100-$125 ea ~ MOC: $20-$30 ea

Series 5: Blood Spattered Jezebel, One-of-a-Kind

Photo courtesy of www.plmk.com

This doll is one of five of the RAREST Series 5 black & white or Mystery dolls made. Only one of each of the dolls was made with colored blood spattering. The dolls look like characters from an old black & white movie, spattered with red paint to look like blood. The four other bloody dolls are Hollywood, Vincent Vaude, Dahlia, and Siren. This bloody Jezebel was found in the United Kingdom around March 2003. Not only did the owner get lucky enough to find this doll, it also came with a mail away certificate for another one of a kind doll. The mail away doll was a unique handmade "Sadie" doll, seen on the next page. In May 2003, blood spattered Jezebel had an asking price of $1,600 and recently sold for $1,100. The value below is an estimate of what we might sell this doll for in our online store.

One of a Kind Blood Spattered Jezebel: $1,100-$1,500

Very Rare Handmade One-of-a-Kind Mail-away Sadie Doll

Photos courtesy of www.plmk.com

The blood spattered Jezebel seen on the previous page came with a certificate for a greater prize, if the owner mailed it in. Here is what the certificate read: "Your Dolls are dead, And here is a clue, This doll is 1 in 5 in the world, So lucky are you, The note you now read, is a symbol of treasure, Mail this letter to me, And receive further pleasure, MEZ." Damien and Ed created this handmade Sadie, she is one of a kind, comes with a bouquet of red roses and a black coffin. Her coffin is not sealed but rather an open one like the earlier handmade dolls. Sadie was for sale at an online auction in February 2004, she DID NOT sell and the reserve amount was undisclosed. The highest bid posted was $431.00; she later sold for $645.00. The estimated value given below is what we might sell this doll for in our online store.

One-of-a-Kind Handmade Sadie Estimated Value: $1,500-$1,600

Series 6: Jinx with Hell Cat

Death Certificate

I hereby certify that on the Seventh day of June, 1913

Jinx

Breaking mirrors and walking under ladders till she died This unlucky kitten used up all of her nine lives

Damien Glonek & Ed Long — Morticians — 06-07-1913 — Date

Living Dead Dolls

84

Photos courtesy of www.plmk.com

Jinx came with a pet named Hell Cat and a death certificate

Photos courtesy of www.wackystacker.com

MSC: $30-$35 ~ MOC: $20-$25

Series 6: Hush with Shriek the Rat

Death Certificate

I hereby certify that on the Twentieth day of December, 1971

Hush

Shy little Hush thought rats were so pretty
So it was her good fortune she lived by the city
It was easy to sneak into the sewer each night
To offer her pets a cheesy delight
But one silly slip landed Hush on her head
It was right there she drowned and the rats were well fed

Damien Glonek & Ed Long — Morticians — 12-20-1971 — Date

Living Dead Dolls

82

Hush came with a pet named Shriek the Rat and a death certificate

Photos courtesy of www.wackystacker.com

MSC: $25-$30 ~ MOC: $15-$20

Series 6: Dottie Rose with Hun the Poodle

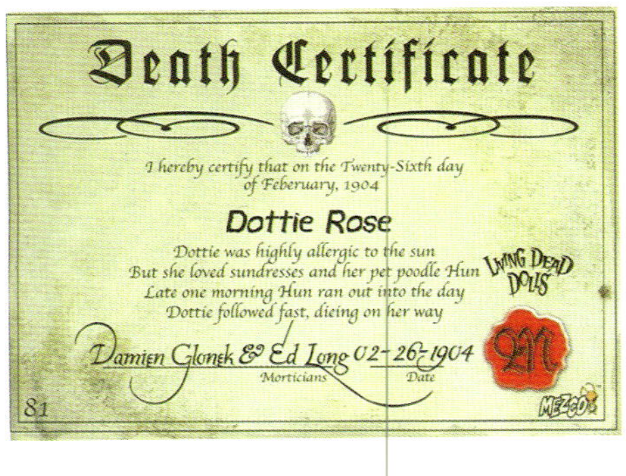

Photos courtesy of www.wackystacker.com

Dottie Rose came with a pet named Hun the Poodle and a death certificate. There were variations made with and without eyebrows. There is no real value difference between the doll either with eyebrows or without eyebrows. This difference however makes the doll in general more collectible among collectors.

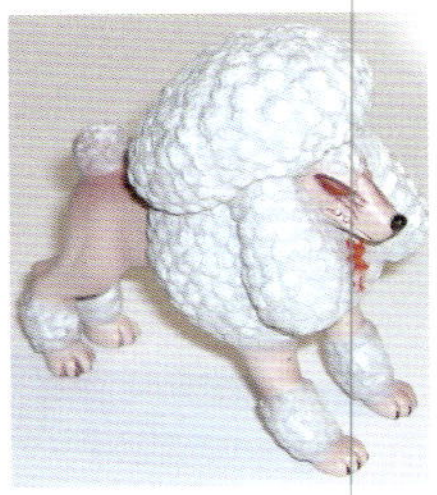

MSC: $25-$35 ~ MOC: $15-$20

Series 6: Isaac Scarecrow with Ole' Crow

Isaac Scarecrow came with a pet Ole' Crow and a death certificate

Photos courtesy of www.wackystacker.com

MSC: $20 to $25 ~ MOC: $10-$15

Series 6: Calico with Muzzy

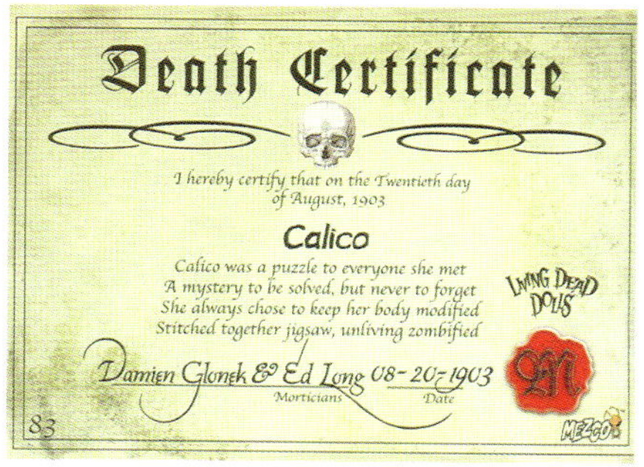

Calico has purple dreadlocks, came with a pet named Muzzy and a death certificate

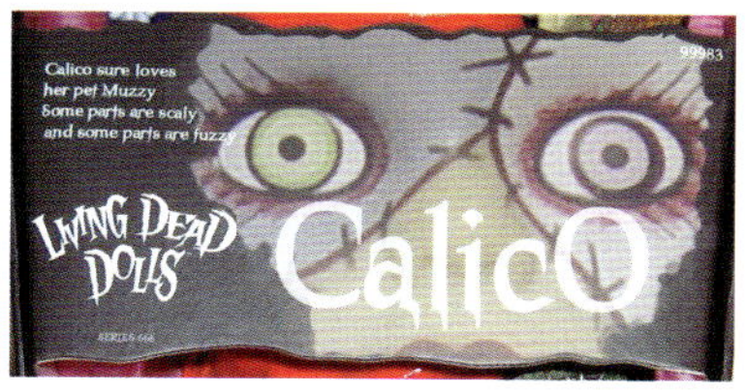

Photos courtesy of www.wackystacker.com

MSC: $25-$35 ~ MOC: $15-$20

Series 6: Revenant with Carrion the Vulture

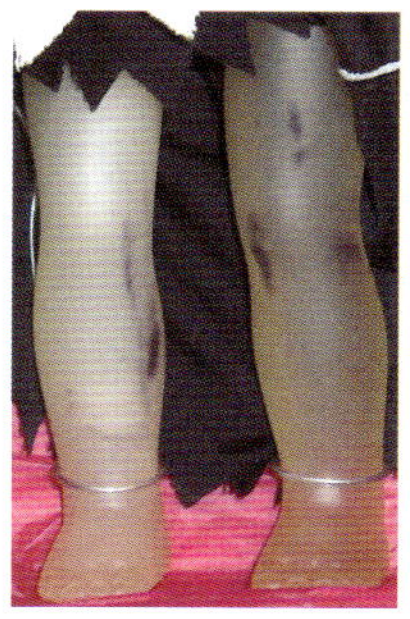

Revenant, first glow in the dark doll, came with a pet named Carrion the Vulture and a death certificate

Photos courtesy of www.wackystacker.com

MSC: $25-$30 ~ MOC: $15-$20

Series 7: Seven Deadly Sins

Series 7 was released as a seven-doll set in May 2004 with an unknown production run. This series was named "The Seven Deadly Sins," with each character being named after a biblical sin. Each doll also comes with definition and "NAME" on the label.

Series 7: Gluttony

Death Certificate

I hereby certify that on the Twenty-ninth day of July, 1974 at 6:30 pm

GLUTTONY

has been pronounced legally deceased.

The excessive food and drink that he craved
Sent this butcher to an early grave
Now trapped in Hell all he can partake
Is being force-fed rats, toads and snakes

Damien Glonek & Ed Long — Morticians — 7-29-1974 — Date

93

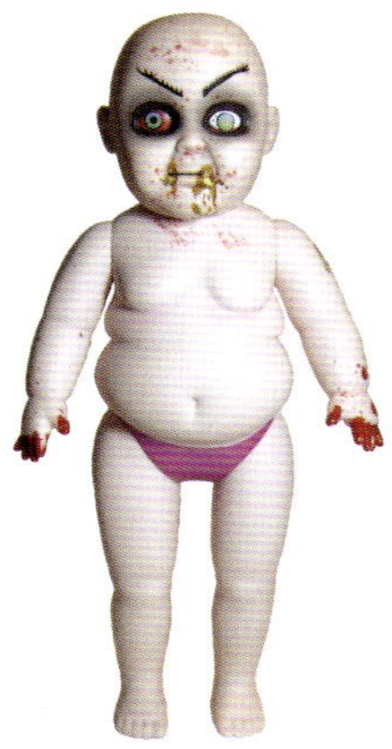

Label Reads: Gluttony 1. Excessive Eating & Drinking, See "Vulgar the Obscene." Gluttony introduced a new body and head style and included a heart tattoo with the word "MEAT" scrolled on a ribbon across his left shoulder. His killer accessories include two knives, meat mallet, human leg bone, and a death certificate.

Photos courtesy of www.wackystacker.com

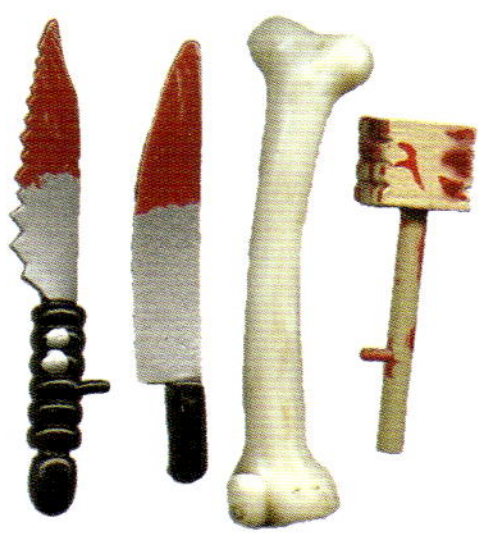

Gluttony MSC: $25-$35 ~ MOC: $15-$20

Series 7: Envy

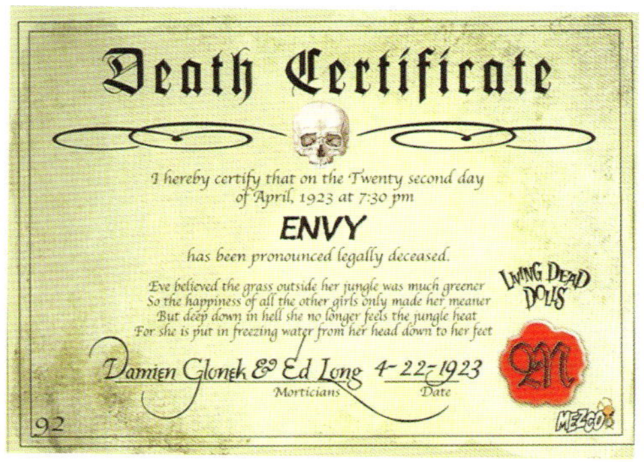

Death Certificate

I hereby certify that on the Twenty second day
of April, 1923 at 7:30 pm

ENVY

has been pronounced legally deceased.

Eve believed the grass outside her jungle was much greener
So the happiness of all the other girls only made her meaner
But deep down in hell she no longer feels the jungle heat
For she is put in freezing water from her head down to her feet

Damien Glonek & Ed Long 4-22-1923
Morticians Date

Living Dead Dolls

92 Mezco

Photos courtesy of
www.wackystacker.com

Envy, also known as Eva-A-Go-Go came with a bone necklace and a death certificate

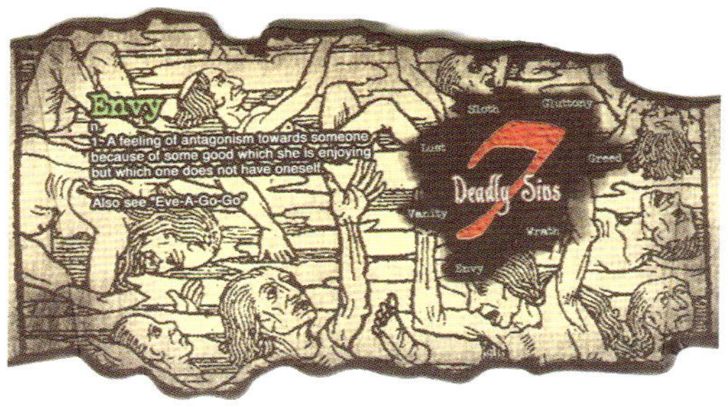

MSC: $25-$30 ~ MOC: $10-$20

Series 7: Greed

Death Certificate

I hereby certify that on the Fourteenth day
of June, 1946 at 2:22 pm

GREED

has been pronounced legally deceased.

Lavish dresses and gems were her only attire
Filling her piggy banks is all she required
Now she is chained to her earthly spoils
To be eternally boiled alive in oils

Damien Glonek & Ed Long 6-14-1946
Morticians Date

Living Dead Dolls

94 Mezco

Greed, also known as Miss McGreedy, came with chains, jewels, piggy bank, and a death certificate

Photos courtesy of
www.wackystacker.com

MSC: $25-$35 ~ MOC: $15-$20

Series 7: Lust

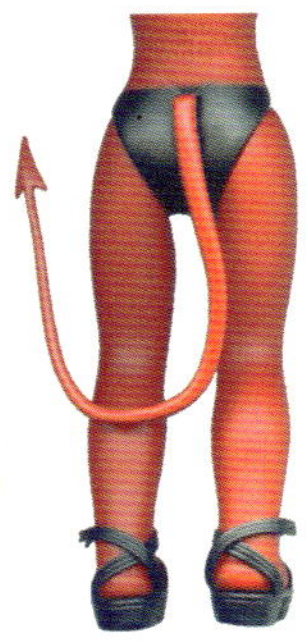

Photos courtesy of
www.wackystacker.com

Lust, also known as Mistress Demonika, came with a whip and a death certificate

MSC: $30-$35 ~ MOC: $15-$20

Series 7: Sloth

Sloth, also known as Bed Time Sadie, came with *Dante's Bedtime Stories* book and a death certificate

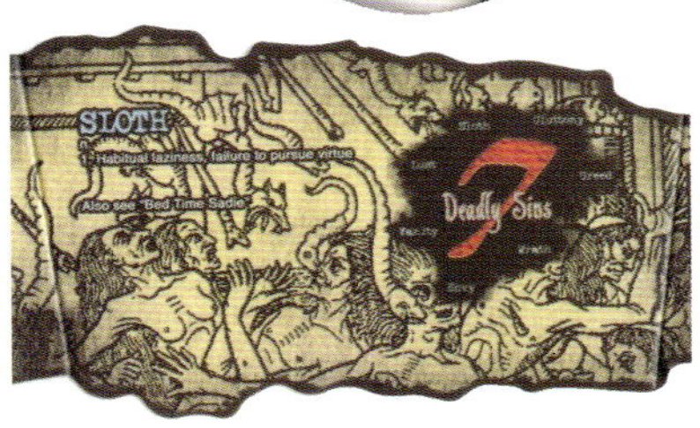

Photos courtesy of
www.wackystacker.com

MSC: $30-$35 ~ MOC: $15-$20

Series 7: Vanity

Death Certificate

I hereby certify that on the Twenty-ninth day
of August, 1958 at 5:38 pm

VANITY

has been pronounced legally deceased.

Madame Dysmorphic was never attractive enough
So Dr. Dedwin called her bluff
He cut her & stitched her & made her so pretty
She died on the table, oh what a pity

Damien Glonek & Ed Long — 8-29-1958
Morticians — Date

Living Dead Dolls

96

Vanity, also known as Madame Dismorphic, came with an "I Am Pretty" skull mirror and a death certificate

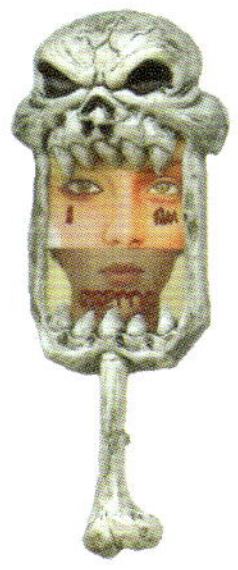

Photos courtesy of
www.wackystacker.com

MSC: $25-$30 ~ MOC: $15-$20

Series 7: Wrath

Death Certificate

I hereby certify that on the Fifth day
of April, 1908 at 8:00 pm

WRATH

has been pronounced legally deceased.

Bad Bette Jane was often red in the face
A screaming little spoiled rotten disgrace
Always allowing her rage to thrive
So now she must be dismembered alive

Damien Glonek & Ed Long — 4-5-1908
Morticians — Date

Living Dead Dolls

91

Wrath, also known as Bad Betty Jane, came with a lollipop & death certificate

Photos courtesy of
www.wackystacker.com

MSC: $25-$35 ~ MOC: $15-$20

Exclusives:

Club Mez Mr. Graves & Abigail Crane

Mr. Graves

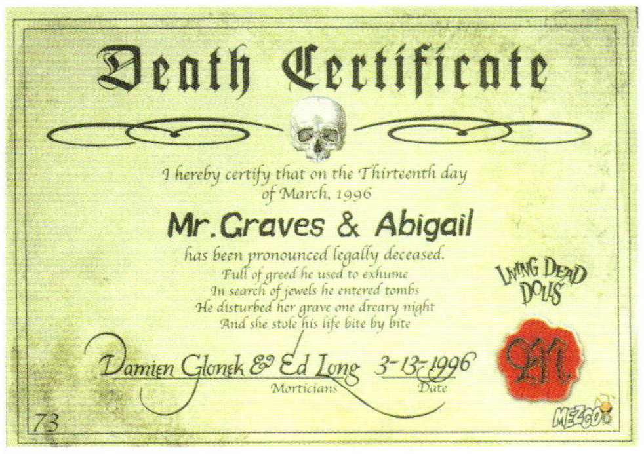

Abigail Crane

Mezco Toyz™ released Mr. Graves & Abigail Crane as a two-pack Club Mez Exclusive available by joining their online club for $40. Accessories included in this double coffin set were a shovel, death certificate, and a headstone that read; "Abigail Crane, 1965-1973, She hated life and all its terms, now she's dead, just food for worms".

Photos courtesy of www.wackystacker.com

Each of the dolls comes with a death certificate, wrapped in burgundy colored cloth ribbon as seen above. Mr. Grave & Abigail Crane were limited to 3,000 pieces and originally sold for $59.99 in September 2002. Abigail Crane was later cast into an 18" porcelain doll also offered as a Club Mez Exclusive.

MSC $70-$90 ~ MOC: $40-$50

Exclusives:
Tower Records Died & Doom

Death Certificate

I hereby certify that on the Ninth day
of August, 1969, at 12:01 A.M.,

Died & Doom

has been pronounced legally deceased.

No wedding night bliss for this bride and groom.
That murdered each other on their honeymoon.
They hated one another right from the start.
But not even death could keep them apart.

Damien Glonek & Ed Long — Morticians
8-9-69 — Date

Postmortem Marriage License

I hereby certify that on the Ninth day
of August, 1969, at 12:02 A.M.,

As punishment for the sins of their crime,
they shall remain together till the end of time.
It is hereby pronounced that this bride and groom
be wed into blasphemy as

Died & Doom

Witnesses: Sadie
Witnesses: Sin
Signed by: Sinister Minister
Date: 8-9-69

Died & Doom was a Tower Records Exclusive. Included in this two-pack was a death certificate, postmortem marriage license, "just murdered" sign, and a bloody cake spatula that fits perfectly into a slot in Died's chest. Limited to 3,996 pieces this set originally sold for $49.99 in May 2001.

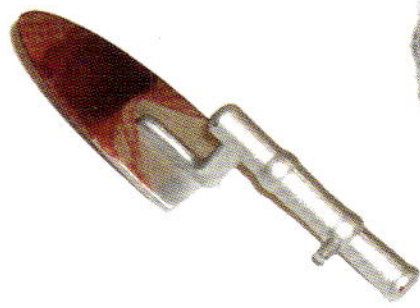

Photos courtesy of www.wackystacker.com

MSC: $160-$190 ~ MOC: $100-$120

Exclusives:
Tower Records Hazel & Hattie

Photos courtesy of Stephen Scweckendieck

Hazel & Hattie was a Tower Records Exclusive. Included in this twin pack were the joined Siamese twins, carnival style poster, and a death certificate. A single shoulder pin joined the twins. Limited to 3,996 pieces, this set originally sold for $49.99 in May 2002.

Death Certificate

I hereby certify that on the Sixth day
of January, 1969, at 6:13 P.M.,

Hazel and Hattie

has been pronounced legally deceased.

Hazel and Hattie were born one of a kind
Hattie died suddenly before their time
Hazel wasn't ready to accept death with her
So Hattie arose to bond them by murder

Damien Glonek & Ed Long — Morticians
1-6-1969 — Date

MSC: $180-$200 ~ MOC: $100-$120

Exclusives: Toy2R Sinister Minister & Bad Habit

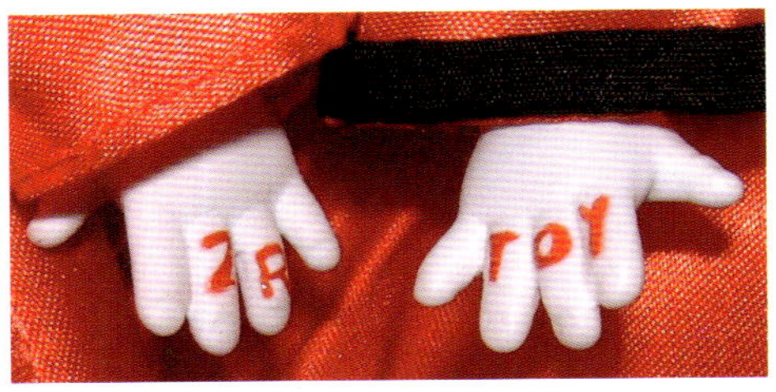

Photos courtesy of Stephen Scweckendieck

Sinister Minister & Bad Habit (red version) originally sold as a two pack Toy2R Exclusive available in Hong Kong only in October 2001. Individually numbered and limited to 999 sets, each had a numbered Toy2R logo skull sticker in the lower right hand corner on the front of the coffin. The set came with rosary beads, incense burner and a death certificate. The fingers on this set read TOY on the right hand and 2R on the left hand. The lower the production numbers on the set the higher the value. If the dolls have been opened, the skull sticker will be intact on the cover.

MSC: $300 (higher #) to $40 (lower #) ~ MOC: $150-$180

Exclusives:
Spencer Gifts Sinister Minister & Bad Habit

Death Certificate

I hereby certify that on the Twenty-fifth day of December, 1966, at 12:00 A.M.,

Sinister Minister & Bad Habbit

has been pronounced legally deceased.
Righteously struck down by lightning.
They rose again fast and frightening.
This blasphemous boy and demented sister.
Have a habit that's bad and a sermon quite sinister

Damien Glonek & Ed Long — Morticians
12-25-66 — Date

Sinister Minister & Bad Habit in black was the first or original set produced as a Spencer Gifts Exclusive two-pack. All three sets had identical accessories as seen with the red set on the previous page. Included were rosary beads, incense burner, and a death certificate. This set however was limited to 3,996 pieces and originally sold for $59.99 in August 2001.

Photos courtesy of Stephen Schweckendieck and www.wackystacker.com

MSC: $80-$120 ~ MOC: $40-$50

Exclusives:
Spencer Gifts Sinister Minster & Bad Habit

Photos courtesy of Stephen Schweckendieck and www.wackystacker.com

The original black set was so popular that Spencer Gifts reordered another set, this time in white robes. Both sets being identical with different colored outfits, but they also have slight differences in the eye colors and packaging tissue. The hands on both sets are also identical and read LOVE & HATE as seen below. Limited to 3,996 pieces this set originally sold for $59.99 in December 2001.

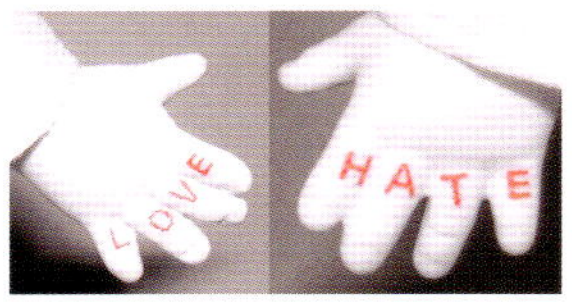

MSC: $80-$120 ~ MOC: $40-$60

Exclusives:
Diamond Comics Doctor Deadwin & Nurse Necro

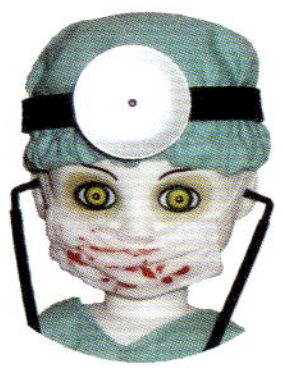

Dr. Deadwin and Nurse Necro were a Diamond Comics Previews Exclusive two-pack. The Doctor came with a bloody mask, stethoscope, and headgear while his Nurse had painted red and white stockings with a plastic dress and hat. Limited to 4,000 pieces this set originally sold for $49.99 in July 2003.

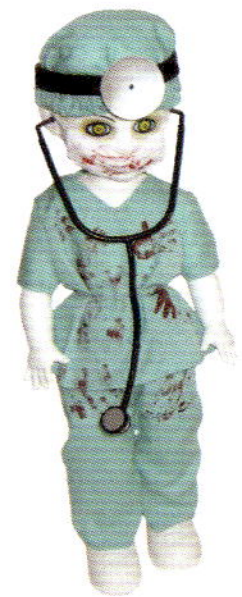

MSC: $50-$60 ~ MOC: $20-$30

Photos courtesy of
www.wackystacker.com

Exlcusives:
Tower Records Psycho-Billies

Billy & Jilly were a Tower Records Exclusive two-pack. These were the first dolls to have extensive tattoos and sunglasses. This set comes with ornate belt buckles and Billy has a wallet with a real chain attached. Limited to 3,600 pieces this set originally sold for $49.99 in September 2003.

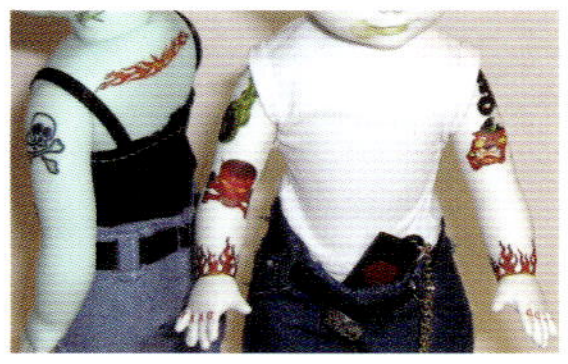

Photos courtesy of
www.wackystacker.com

MSC: $40-$60 ~ MOC: $20-$30

Exclusives:
Hot Topic Tragedy & Misery

Tragedy

Misery & Tragedy Mini 2 pack

Misery

Tragedy, a Hot Topic Exclusive, originally came with red tissue in August 2002. In the middle of production Hot Topic asked to change the tissue to purple. There are said to be less purple tissue then red. Tragedy came with a coffin purse & death certificate. Tragedy needed a boyfriend, thus Misery was released in August 2003.

Photos courtesy of Stephen Schweckendieck and www.wackystacker.com

Misery came with a skull necklace and death certificate. Both Tragedy and Misery originally sold for $28. Released in March 2004 was a very adorable mini two-pack with an original price of $15.99. Production runs are unknown. A new Hot Topic exclusive named Captain Bonney the Pirate is scheduled for release in October 2004.

Tragedy (red tissue) MIC: $50-60~MOC: $30-$40
(purple tissue) MIC: $50-60 ~ MOC: $30-$40
Misery MIC: $35-$40~MOC: $20-$25 Mini
Tragedy & Misery 2 pack MIC: $20-$25~MOC: $10-$15

Exclusive:

Close Up (Germany) Walpurgis

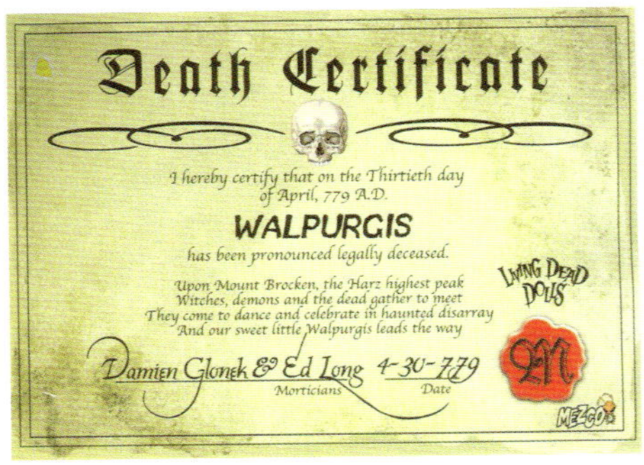

Walpurgis is a German Exclusive made for a company called Close Up. This witch came with a creepy removable goat's mask, pentagram necklace, and a death certificate. The photo top left is the prototype for this doll. In my research, I have found many photos released by Mezco Toyz™ are of the prototype dolls. This doll is hard to find in the U.S., however, you can find them at online auctions or specialty stores like *www.wackystacker.com*. Limited to 5,000 pieces and originally sold for $69.99 in May 2004.

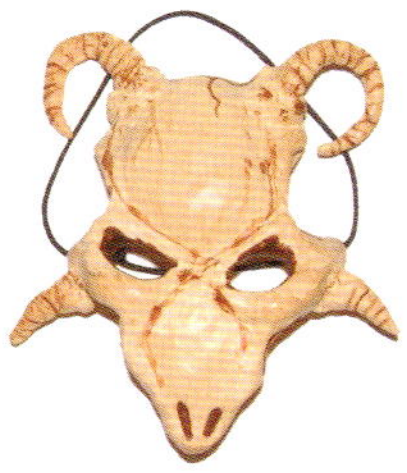

Photos courtesy of Stephen Schweckendieck and www.wackystacker.com

MSC: $60-$70 ~ MOC: $40-$50

Exclusive:

Star Images (United Kingdom) Jack the Ripper

Jack the Ripper was a United Kingdom Exclusive made for a company called Star Images, and fashioned after a real murderer that was never caught. This bloody doll came with a bloody knife, and a death certificate. Also hard to find in the U.S., limited to 4,000 pieces and originally sold for $49.99 in August 2003.

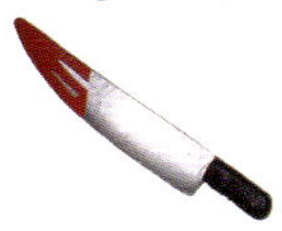

Photos courtesy of Stephen Schweckendieck and www.wackystacker.com

MSC: $65-$75 ~ MOC: $40-$50

Exclusive: Diamond Comics Nosferatu & Victim

Nosferatu & Victim were a Diamond Comics Previews Exclusive two-pack, designed after a silent horror movie from 1922. The set came with a black rat, vampire book and poem certificate with autographs. I noticed right away that this set was very similar to Isaac, Hush, & Shriek the Rat from Series 6. The set originally sold for $49.99 in May 2004.

Photos courtesy of Stephen Schweckendieck and www.wackystacker.com

MSC: $60-$70 ~ MOC: $40-$50

Exclusives: Spencer Gifts Cookie

Cookie from Troop 666 was a Spencer Gifts Exclusive. This little scout came with a box of poisonous Dead Scout Cookies and death certificate. Cookie created some controversy among non-collectors. Limited to 3,996 pieces and originally sold for $27.99 in September 2003.

Photos courtesy of Stephen Schweckendieck and www.wackystacker.com

MCS: $50-$60 ~ MOC: $30-$40

Exclusives:
Tower Records The Great Zombini

Zombini

Viv

The Great Zombini and his lovely assistant Viv, short for vivisection. The twin-pack set, made exclusively for Tower Records, was released June 2004 and limited to less than 4,000 pieces. The set came with a bloody saw so Zombini could perform his magic trick cutting Viv in half exposing her guts. This was the first action set produced and originally sold for $49.99.

Photos courtesy of Stephen Schweckendieck and www.wackystacker.com

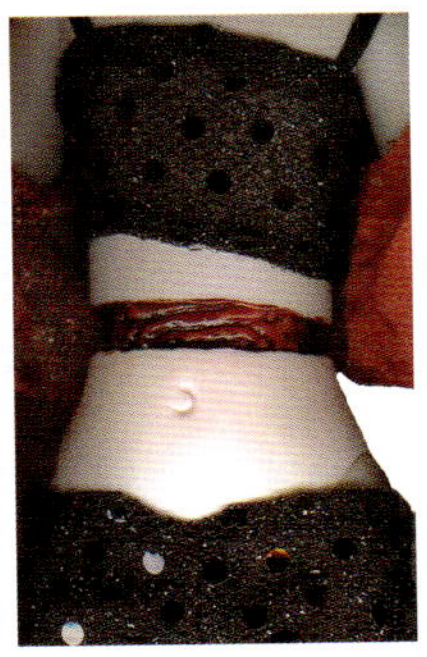

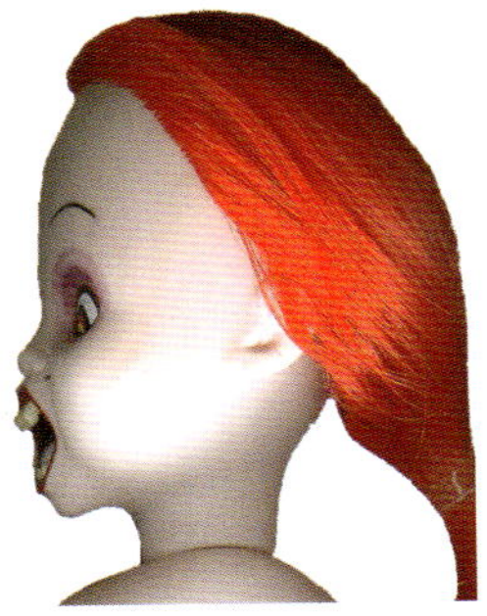

The Great Zombini MSC: $50-$60 ~ MOC: $40-$50

Exclusives:

Marz Distribution Hemlock & Honey

Hemlock & Honey, also known as Trick & Treat, were released August 2004 and limited to less than 3,996 pieces. It is a Marz Distribution exclusive and one of the most bizarre and unique sets produced to date. I love this twin-pack, which includes removable Halloween masks and pumpkin buckets. It is obvious that these kids live a scary life everyday until All Hallows Eve when they put on their masks and become somewhat normal. The masks feature rooted hair, which covers up the hideous looks of these beauties. Small retailers carried this set and it retailed for as little as $39.99.

Death Certificate

I hereby certify that on the
Thirty first day of October, 2003

Hemlock and Honey

have been pronounced legally deceased.

One gloomy night gathering candy
Their poisoned sweets were unforeseen
Left to wander the streets forever
They treat every night now like its Halloween

Damien Glonek & Ed Long — Morticians
10-31-2003 — Date

Living Dead Dolls

55

Photos courtesy of www.wackystacker.com

Hemlock & Honey MSC: $50-$60 ~ MOC: $40-$50

Exclusives:

Toy2R & Club Mez Penny

Club Mez Penny

Toy2R Penny

The original Penny produced was a promotional doll for Toy2R & Easy Finder companies in Hong Kong. This exclusive, blood-spattered doll has brown hair and white clothes. As with the Toy2R red Sinister set, the fingers on Penny read TOY on the right hand and 2R on the left hand. Released June 2001 and limited to 666 pieces, each doll was hand-numbered and available in Hong Kong only. The lower the hand signed numbers the more the doll will be worth.

Photos courtesy of www.wackystacker.com

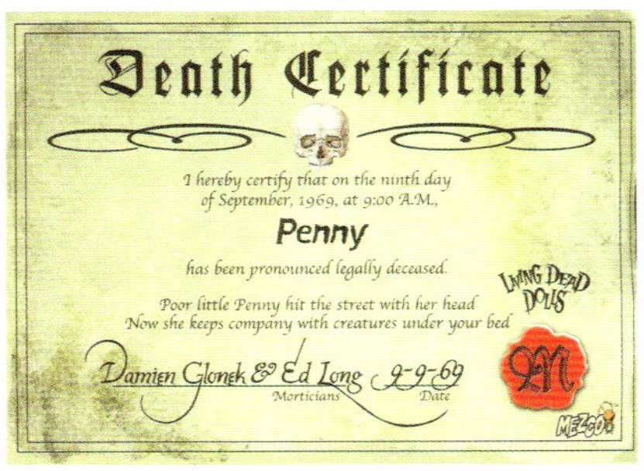

Death Certificate

I hereby certify that on the ninth day of September, 1969, at 9:00 A.M.

Penny

has been pronounced legally deceased.

Poor little Penny hit the street with her head
Now she keeps company with creatures under your bed

Damien Glonk & Ed Long — Mortician
9-9-69 — Date

The original purchase price of Toy2R Penny is unknown. The second Penny released was as a Club Mez Exclusive. Limited to 3,000 pieces, it originally sold for $30 in December 2001. She came with bright orange hair & black clothes. Both dolls came with a bloody hatchet and a death certificate. If the dolls have been opened, the hand written number will be gone and there is no way of knowing what the production number was.

Toy2R Penny MSC: $800-$1000 ~ MOC: $200-$300 Club Mez Penny MSC: $70-$90 ~ MOC: $40-$50

Exclusives:

Comic-Con Blue & Blood Spattered Eggzorcist

The Blue Eggzorcist was made especially for the Comic-Con Convention in San Diego, California, in July 2003. It was limited to 3,000 pieces, came sealed and covered with a black plastic body bag. 100 of the dolls were blood-spattered, a fact that was hidden behind the body bags. The coffin had to be open to remove the body bag and find out whether or not there was a bloody doll. Collectors were limited to purchasing six dolls only for $40 each. Accessories included are a pink roach, basket, and death certificate, which reads the same as the series one doll.

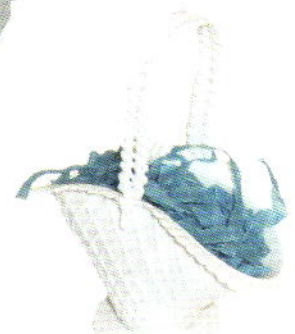

Photos courtesy of www.wackystacker.com

Many collectors opened their dolls right at the show and had their dolls autographed, as seen above. I have found some of the blood-spattered dolls autographed with the words "Real Bloody!" This way future collectors would know that the doll was authentic, thus REAL. When purchasing this doll use extreme caution and look for the autographs. Because they had to be opened, the value of the doll is not as high as if it were a sealed doll like Toy2R Penny. There are several different prices for this doll as follows.

Blue Eggzorcist: Mint Sealed w/ Body Bag: $70-$80 ~ Mint Opened Doll Not Removed: $70-$80 Autographed Mint Opened Doll Not Removed: $100-$120 ~ Autographed w/ Mez Mint Opened Doll Not Removed: $120-$150 ~ Mint Opened Doll Removed: $40-$50 ~ Autographed Mint Opened Blood Spattered Doll Limited to 100 pieces: $700-$800

Exclusives:

San Diego Comic-Con Jack & Jill

Four different twin-pack sets of Jack & Jill were produced and released in July 2004. This black and white set was released as a San Diego Comic-Con exclusive limited to 1,300 pieces. The dolls came sealed in black plastic body bags with a bucket of blood and autographed poem.

Photos courtesy of www.wackystacker.com

Randomly packed inside the sealed body bags were 200 blood-spattered glow in the dark variations. Since the dolls had to be opened to find out if there was a variation inside the price given below is for an open set of dolls. You can expect to pay around the same price for a sealed set.

San Diego Comic-Con Jack & Jill limited to 1,300 pcs ~ MOC: $80-$100

Exclusives:
SDCC Glow-in-the-Dark Blood-Spattered Jack & Jill

The San Diego Comic-Con glow-in-the-dark blood-spattered Jack & Jill variation was limited to 200 pieces. The plastic dolls glow in the dark, have a greenish tint and are spattered with red paint, which looks like blood. The blood spatter is on the face, arms, legs, and clothing. The dolls' backs each have a unique mark, a duplicate to the logo on Nurse Necro's hat.

Photos courtesy of
www.wackystacker.com

Fake dolls do exist so use extreme caution when purchasing this set of dolls. The best authenticity test is to check and see if the dolls glow in the dark by holding them up to bright light then put them in the dark. They will glow bright green. Make sure the dolls are not painted with glow-in-the-dark paint and that the blood-spatter does not rub off.

San Diego Comic-Con Glow/Spatter Jack & Jill
limited to 200 pieces ~ MOC: $600-$800

Exclusives:
Club Mez Jack & Jill

Club Mez Jack & Jill were produced and released in August 2004. This black and red set was exclusive to their online club, limited to 1,300 pieces, with an original selling price of $69. This set has not been fully sold out as the SDCC set therefore it is harder to come by on the secondary market and has a slightly higher value.

Photos courtesy of
www.wackystacker.com

Both regular sets of dolls have white bodies. The differences are the color of the clothes, eyes and tissue paper inside the coffins. Do not be confused by the blood running down Jack's face; it is not the blood-spattered version.

San Diego Comic-Con Jack & Jill limited to 1,300 pieces ~ MOC: $100-$130

Exclusives:
Club Mez Glow-in-the-Dark Blood-Spattered Jack & Jill

The Club Mez glow-in-the-dark blood-spattered Jack & Jill variation was limited to 200 pieces. This version is much more difficult to find than the other Jack & Jill sets. Collectors were limited to how many dolls they could purchase from the online club, which in turn limits the supply on the secondary market.

Photos courtesy of www.wackystacker.com

You can expect to pay around 20-30% more for the Club Mez glow variation. The color of this set when not exposed to light is a pale almost translucent white color. The example above shows the back of Jack glowing and the back of Jill not glowing for comparison.

Club Mez Glow/Spatter Jack & Jill limited to 200 pieces ~ MOC: $700-$900

Living Dead Dollies:

Lilith

Photos courtesy of www.wackystacker.com

Living Dead Dollies™ Lilith made her debut at the San Diego Comic-Con in July 2004 and was limited to 1,000 pieces. There were two Lilith exclusives available at the show to include a regular and a bloody version as seen above. The dolls are the baby versions of the original 10″ doll. They possess the same unique style and measure approx. 9″ tall. They come with a headband, removable outfit, and diaper, and came packaged in black plastic body bags concealing 200 blood-spattered Lilith dollies. They were also available at Club Mez and sold out within hours for $25 each.

SDCC/Club Mez Lilith Dollie MIP: $40-$50 ~ Autographed SDCC/Club Mez Lilith Dollie MINT: $100-$120 ~ Blood Spattered Lilith Dollie Limited to 200 pieces MINT: $200-$300

Living Dead Ragdolls:

Moana — Orchid — Jeepers

Moana

Orchid

Photos courtesy of www.wackystacker.com

Jeepers

Living Dead Ragdolls™ are a new line of 12" plush dolls released in July 2004. Included are Moana, Orchid, and Jeepers. Each doll comes with removable outfits and coffin-shaped swing tags with creepy poems. You can expect to pay $15 to $20 each.

Exclusive Ragdolls:

Dementia

Photos courtesy of Kristy Pickup and www.wackystacker.com

Dementia is a 12" Rag Doll released as a Comic-Con San Diego exclusive in July 2004 and available through Club Mez for $25. This doll came packaged in a black poly body bag and was limited to 700 pieces. One hundred plush dolls were rare variations with gray & black hair.

Dementia MINT: $25-$40 ~ Dementia Variation limited to 100 pieces MINT: $100-$150

Club Mez Exclusive Plush:

Bed Time Sadie

Photos courtesy of www.wackystacker.com

Bed Time Sadie with Deddy Bear was released as a Club Mez Exclusive in August 2003. Limited to 2,400 pieces, she stands 13" tall, has a vinyl head and hands, stuffed body, rooted hair, and removable cap with glow-in-the-dark skull outfit. When you lay her down her eyes will close; pick her up and her eyes will open. Deddy is a soft plush measuring 4" tall. Originally sold for $33 and came packed in a padded envelope with the Club Mez logo.

Bed Time Sadie Plush w/ Deddy Bear MIP: $60-$70 ~ Mint Opened: $40-$50

Porcelain Series:

Posey & Club Mez Abigail Crane

The porcelain dolls are 18" tall with plush bodies, porcelain head, hands, and feet. The dolls are hand-painted and based on the smaller original version dolls. Each came packaged in a large cardboard simulated wooden coffin. Posey was limited to 4,600 pieces and originally sold for $49.99 in December 2003.

Certificate of Authenticity
Porcelain Living Dead Doll
Posey
It is hereby certified that this is an official porcelain Living Dead Doll
Each doll is hand crafted & hand painted and carries the Living Dead Doll seal of authenticity
This doll is of a limited production run & will not be produced again.
Living Dead Dolls

Photos courtesy of
www.wackystacker.com

Abigail Crane released as a Club Mez Exclusive limited to 1,000 pieces with an original selling price of $79.99. A hand-numbered "Certificate of Authenticity" is included with each doll. These dolls look so much like a small Linda Blair from the 1970s movie "The Exorcist."

Certificate of Authenticity
Porcelain Living Dead Doll
ABIGAIL CRANE
It is hereby certified that this is an official porcelain Living Dead Doll
Each doll is hand crafted & hand painted and carries the Living Dead Doll seal of authenticity
This doll is of a limited production run & will not be produced again.
Living Dead Dolls

Posey MSC: $40-50 ~ MOC: $30-$40 ~ Abigail Crane MSC: $140-$160 ~ MOC: $100-$120

Fashion Victims Series 1:

Kitty

Photos courtesy of www.wackystacker.com

Fashion Victims are a very risqué version based on the original 10" dolls. The dolls measure 13" tall made of rubber, have wire inside the arms & legs, and easily bend for posing. The dolls come with a change of clothes, accessories, a unique "Deadmate Data Sheet," and pin-up poster on the reverse side. Series one released in October 2003 with an original selling price of $20-$25 each. Production numbers are unknown.

Kitty MSC: $20 to $25 ~ MOC: $10-$15

Fashion Victims Series 1:

Lilith

Photos courtesy of
www.wackystacker.com

DEADMATE DATA SHEET

LIVING DEAD DOLLS
FASHION VICTIMS

NAME: *Lilith*

YEARS DECEASED: *I may be dead but I don't kiss & smell*

SIGN: *Anything but the cross*

POST MORTEM GOALS: *Keep on sucking*

TURN ONS: *Soil I was buried in, bloody kisses, a hearts final beat*

TURN OFFS: *The sun, guys with wood in their hand*

IDEAL NIGHTMARE: *To turn bony little poser dolls into cattle for my feeding*

My Sunday Best.

Stepping Out For A Bite.

Lilith came in three different variations, a regular or non-blood-spattered version, a blood-spattered version (seen above), and a Chiller Theatre exclusive. The regular version, seen in the pin-up poster above, has no blood on her mouth or body. The clothes and accessories are the same. There is a slight value difference for the blood-spattered version and the production numbers are unknown.

Lilith MSC: \$20 to \$25 ~ MOC: \$10-\$15 ~ Blood Spattered Lilith MSC: \$40 to \$60 ~ MOC: \$20-\$25

Fashion Victims Series 1:
Sadie

Photos courtesy of
www.wackystacker.com

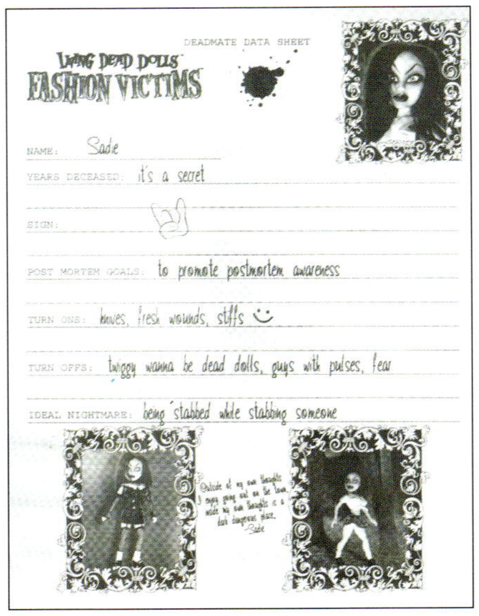
DEADMATE DATA SHEET

LIVING DEAD DOLLS
FASHION VICTIMS

NAME: Sadie

YEARS DECEASED: it's a secret

SIGN:

POST MORTEM GOALS: to promote postmortem awareness

TURN ONS: knives, fresh wounds, stiffs :)

TURN OFFS: twiggy wanna be dead dolls, guys with pulses, fear

IDEAL NIGHTMARE: being stabbed while stabbing someone

Sadie is the most popular Fashion Victim among collectors, which has increased her value above the other dolls. The Sadie doll has been released in more variations than any other character of Living Dead Dolls™. You can also find her on the portfolios, t-shirts, pin back buttons, barware, and more.

Sadie MSC: $30 to $35 ~ MOC: $20-$25

Fashion Victims Series 1: Sheena

Photos courtesy of
www.wackystacker.com

DEADMATE DATA SHEET

LIVING DEAD DOLLS FASHION VICTIMS

NAME: SHEENA

YEARS DECEASED: WHAT EVER- PISS OFF!

SIGN: Ⓐ

POST MORTEM GOALS: TO SMASH YA BLOODY FACE IN - YA HIPPIE

TURN ONS: I'M HORNY FOR VIOLENCE

TURN OFFS: BORING- NEXT!

IDEAL NIGHTMARE: TO STAGE DIVE WITH A CHAINSAW INTO A CROWD AT A "DEAD" CONCERT

The Fashion Victims come with unique clothing and their names definitely suit them. Overall, I found changing the clothes to be quite difficult on the Fashion Victims. The hands & feet are removable and snap into place with button type ends, which helped somewhat. However, the combination of rubber bodies and skintight clothes made changing the clothes difficult. Series 2 Fashion Victims are scheduled for release in October 2004 and will include Lulu, Inferno, Sybil, and Hollywood.

Sheena MSC: $20 to $25 ~ MOC: $10-$15

Fashion Victims Series 1:
Chiller Theatre Lilith Exclusive

Photos courtesy of www.wackystacker.com

This Fashion Victim was a promotional blood spattered version of Lilith in a red outfit available only at the 13th Annual Chiller Theatre Convention in October 2003. Limited to 666 pieces and originally sold for $40.

Chiller Lilith Exclusive MIB: $60-$70 ~ MOP: $20-$40 ~ Autographed Chiller Lilith Exclusive MIB: $80-$100

Series 1 Minis:

Damien — Sin — Eggzorcist — Sadie — Posey

Photos courtesy of www.wackystacker.com

A duplicate miniature series was produced of the larger 10" dolls in August 2002. Packaged in miniature coffins each mini doll measures 4" tall. Unlike the large dolls, the minis have ball joints on their shoulders for greater movement. The dolls sold separately for $6-$7 each.

Set of 5 MSC: $50-$60 ~ Singles MSC: $12-$15 ~ Singles MOC: $5-$6

Series 2 Minis:

Kitty — Lou Sapphire — Deabra Ann — Lizzie Borden — Bedtime Sadie

Photos courtesy of www.wackystacker.com

Series 2 Minis was also an exact duplicate, with the featured introduction of the "Bedtime Sadie" doll seen in the center. School Time Sadie of series two was released in a Stationary Set made exclusively for Marz Distribution. Series 2 was released in March 2003 and originally sold for $6-$7 each.

Set of 5 MSC: $30-$35 ~ Singles MSC: $10-$12 ~ Singles MOC: $4-$5

Series 3 Minis:
Lottie — Lilith — Bride of Valentine — Sheena — Schitzo

Photos courtesy of www.wackystacker.com

Series 3 Minis are an exact duplicate of the series three 10" dolls. Although none of the mini dolls come with accessories like the larger dolls they are just as highly detailed in the paint & clothing. Series three minis released in October 2003 and originally sold for $6-$7 each.

Set of 5 MSC: $25-$30 ~ Singles MSC: $8-$9 ~ Singles MOC: $3-$4

Series 4 Minis:
Dr. Deadwin & Nurse Necro — Died & Doom — Penny

Photos courtesy of www.wackystacker.com

Series 4 Minis are a mix of different exclusives originally produced in the 10" dolls over the past few years. All mini dolls each come with a small hangman's noose made of string on one end and a metal clip on the other. The noose doubles as a key chain. Series four minis released June 2004 and originally sold for $6-$7 each. Production numbers are unknown for the mini series dolls.

Set of 5 MSC: $25-$30 ~ Singles MSC: $6-$7 ~ Singles MOC: $2-$3

Spencer Gifts Exclusive

Mini Mausoleum:

Damien — Posey — Sin —
Eggzorcist — Sadie — Red Sinister
Minister & Bad Habit

Photos courtesy of www.wackystacker.com

Spencer Gifts Exclusive set of 7 mini dolls, released December 2002, originally sold for $59.99. This set included the Series 1 Minis with the bonus being the red Sinister Minister & Bad Habit, which could only be obtain by purchasing this set.

Spencer Gifts Mausoleum I MSC: $70-$90 ~ MOC: $20-$30

Spencer Gifts Exclusive Mini Mausoleum:

Schitzo — Lilith — Lottie — Sheena —
Bride of Valentine — Red Bedtime Sadie — Blue Eggzorcist

Photos courtesy of www.wackystacker.com

Spencer Gifts Exclusive set of 7 Mini dolls, released November 2003, originally sold for $59.99. This set included the Series 3 Minis with the bonus being the blue Eggzorcist & red Bedtime Sadie, which could only be obtained by purchasing this set. Production run was 3,000 sets of each mausoleum set.

Spencer Gifts Mausoleum II MSC: $60-$70 ~ MOC: $20-$30

FX Show Exclusive:
Mini Bloody Eggzorcist

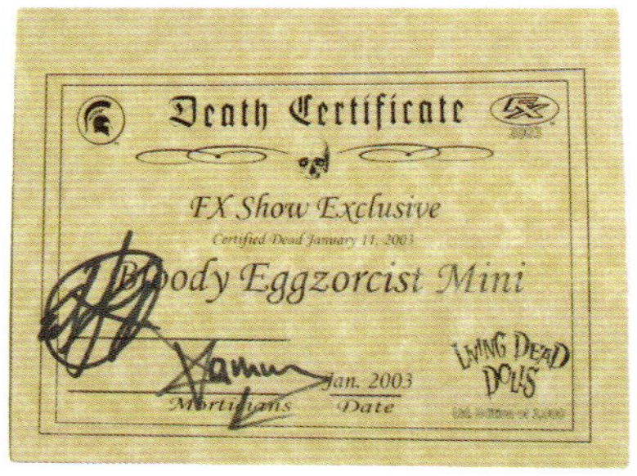

Photos courtesy of
www.wackystacker.com

Produced exclusively for Marz Distribution for the FX Show in Florida, a mini blood-spattered Eggzorcist, limited to 3,000 pieces, was released in January 2003 and originally sold for $20. The blood-spattered Eggzorcist is the only mini doll that comes with an autographed death certificate. Damien and Ed hand signed each certificate.

FX Eggzorcist w/ Certificate: MSC: $20-$25 ~ w/o Certificate MSC: $10-$15

Marz Distribution Exclusive:
Stationary Set with School Time Sadie

Photos courtesy of
www.wackystacker.com

School Time Sadie of Series 2 included in this "The Stationary Set To Die For" and made exclusively for Marz Distribution. This set was limited to 3,000 pieces released in August 2002. Other items included in the set: coroner's zip-up body bag, logo and doll stickers, bloody ruler, white ink pen, pencils, sharpener, tombstone eraser, and black paper and envelopes. The set originally sold for $30.

Sealed Set MSC: $20-$30 ~ School Time Sadie: $8-$12

Toy2R Exclusive Minis:
Sadie – Posey – Eggzorcist

Left to right: Hong Kong Toy2R 3 pack ~ Japan Toy2R 3 pack Photos courtesy of www.wackystacker.com

The mini three-packs seen above were limited to 999 pieces each and made exclusively for Toy2R. The Hong Kong set was released in December 2001 and available from the retailer in Hong Kong only. The Japan set was released a year later in January 2002 and available from the retailer in Japan only. You can clearly see the differences in the sets above. Below you will see two similar three-pack sets released from Club Mez at almost the same time.

Hong Kong Toy2R MSC: $80-$100 ~ Japan Toy2R MSC: $80-$100

Club Mez Exclusive Minis:
Sadie –Posey – Eggzorcist

Left to right: Hong Kong Club Mez 3 pack ~ Japan Club Mez 3 pack Photos courtesy of www.wackystacker.com

On the heels of the Toy2R sets, the Club Mez Hong Kong set was released in January 2001 and the Japan set in January 2002. These mini three-packs were limited to 500 pieces each with glow-in-the-dark faces and sold exclusively to Club Mez members. In my opinion, the paint used to make the dolls glow made them look creepier than the Toy2R sets. They were packaged in square boxes that had either white or red letters. We are assuming here that the sets from Japan came in the red boxes. The best way to know what you have is to check the faces on the dolls. Besides glowing in the dark the Club Mez dolls have a somewhat yellow tint, a rough feel and creepier look to them. The difference is very apparent, as the glow dolls have exaggerated paint features.

Hong Kong Club Mez MSC: $100-$120 ~ Japan Club Mez MSC: $100-$120

Other Items:

Sadie 3-D Journal – Sadie & Posey Pencil Sharpeners

Photos courtesy of www.wackystacker.com

Mezco Toys™ has released several other collectible items. Included here is a journal with lock, keys, and a white marker pen. On the front is a 3-D picture of Sadie that changes from her human face to her skeleton face when you tilt the book in different directions. 3-D cards and other objects were popular back in the early 1970s and are making their comeback on items like this journal. Next up were two bizarre pencil sharpeners of the Series 1 Sadie & Posey dolls. To sharpen the pencil it is inserted it into the eyeball, making the tongue pop out. The sharpeners come with rooted hair.

Sadie Journal MIP: $10-$15 ~ Sadie/Posey Pencil Sharpener MIP: $10-$12

Other Items:

Board Game

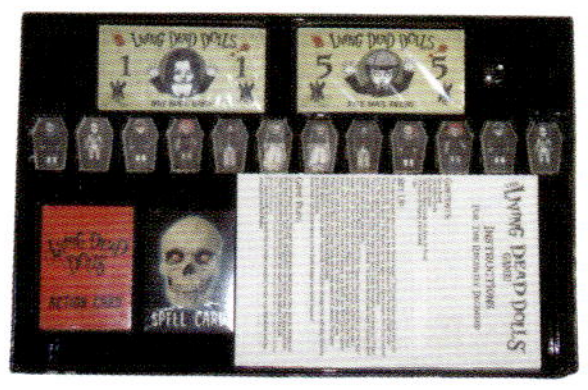

Photos courtesy of www.wackystacker.com

Released simultaneously in 2003 were this board game and the Party Lights on the following page. The game includes 12 paper doll game pieces, action cards, spell cards, play money, and a unique and colorful game board featuring many of the dolls, their tombstones, and walking along paths named Ripper Meadow, Dead Dolls Curve, and the School House. It even has what appear to be Damien and Ed as zombies on the left bottom edge of the board.

Board Game MIB: $20-$25

Other Items:
Posie Tabletop Water Fountain
~ Lottie Notebook

Courtesy of Living Dead Dolls, LLC

A tabletop water fountain was unveiled at the 2003 Toy Fair show. It features Posey emerging from her grave and dribbles blood (colored water) down the front of the tombstone. The fountain measures 10″ tall x 6″ wide x 8″ deep. Pictured on the far right is a notebook with Lottie on the cover. The fountain and notebook were not available for purchase and appeared at the 2003 Toy Fair show only.

Posey Tabletop Fountain: Value Not Available ~ Lottie Note Book: Value Not Available

Other Items:
Party Lights

Photos courtesy of www.wackystacker.com

The Party Lights are the cat's meow of accessories and featured five different doll heads on a string of lights. Included were Kitty, Posey, Lulu, Sadie, and Schitzo heads. The girl dolls came with rooted hair. They were all the same size as the regular dolls heads but instead made with a see-through plastic that made the paint features on the heads show up nicely in the dark. I recommend adding this item to your collection while the prices are reasonable.

Party Lights Set MIB: $25-$30

Other Items:

Limited Edition Collector's Set

Series 1 Trading Cards

Certificate of Authenticity

These Series One Living Dead Dolls cards were produced as a Limited Edition Collectors Set. This set is limited to only 2,500 packs. These trading cards are based upon the Creepy Doll Series, created by Damien Glonek and Ed Long. These Cards were designed and produced by Mediaessence with photography by Jonathan Sevilla.

0190/2500

Living Dead Dolls

The Living Dead Dolls Series is a Copyright © 2002 of Living Dead Dolls, L.L.C. All rights reserved. Made in U.S.A.

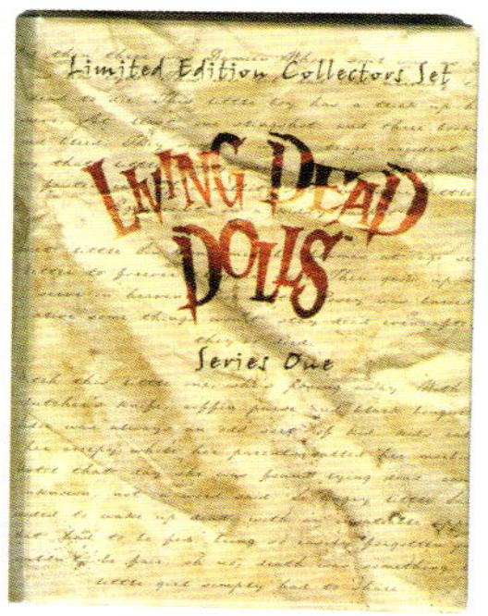

Photos courtesy of www.wackystacker.com

Series 1 Trading Cards came with a numbered certificate of authenticity, and were limited to 2,500 sets. Released in 2002, they were available exclusively at *www.livingdeaddolls.com*. They originally sold for $5.00 plus shipping of $2.00. I found a nice looking framed set of cards, sticker, pin-back button, and Damien's and Ed's autographs at an online auction shortly after the release of the cards with an asking price of $90. The set did not sell. Estimated Value on this framed set would be around $50-$60 in our store.

Collector's Set Series One Trading Cards MIP: $7-$12

Other Items:
Lunch Boxes

Photos courtesy of www.wackystacker.com

The Series 1 tin lunch box depicts the advertisement used to promote the dolls right before their release in 2001. Series 2, seen center, was also released using the advertisement from that series. Club Mez then made available, to its members only, the final lunch box, seen in the last photo. At the time of this writing, the exclusive boxes are available at their online club for $12.99.

Series One Box Mint: $15-$20 ~ Series Two Box Mint: $15-$20 ~ Club Mez Exclusive Box Mint: $13-$15

Other Items:
NECA Head Knockers

Photos courtesy of www.wackystacker.com

NECA Head Knockers™ released these four nodders or bobble heads in 2003. Cast in resin, they stand 7" to 8" tall. Posey and Eggzorcist were released first, soon followed by Lizzie Borden and Lou Sapphire. These have a very high level of detail and are unique and readily available at several online stores.

Posey MIB: $8-$10 ~ Eggzorcist MIB: $8-$10 ~ Lizzie Borden MIB: $8-$10 ~ Lou Sapphire MIB $8-$10

Other Items:
T-shirts – Stickers – Pin-Back Buttons

Photos courtesy of www.wackystacker.com

T-shirts, stickers, and pin back buttons are available at *www.livingdeaddolls.com*. You can sometimes find the older t-shirts at online auctions for around $25-$35. I have found t-shirts with many different logo designs and sayings.

5 year T-shirt New: $15-$20 ~ Sticker & Pin Back Buttons Mint: $1 each ~ Sadie T-shirt New: $15-$20

Other Items:
Barware – Drinking Glasses

Photos courtesy of www.drinkwiththelivingdead.com

Drinking glasses & barware were available in very limited numbers. The glassware was hand-etched in collaboration with Damien and Ed, Mezco Toyz™ and *www.crystaletching.com*. This set is named, "I Ate My Mommy," was featured at the San Diego Comic-Con in July 2003 and can still be purchased at *www.drinkwiththelivingdead.com* for $99.99. Each of the four glasses has a unique saying that tells a story of how Sadie ate her mommy.

I Ate My Mommy Barware Set MIB: $100-$120

Other Items:
Series 1 Barware
Drinking Glasses

Photos courtesy of
www.wackystacker.com

Series 1 barware sets were the first of the three sets released. They were available at the San Diego Comic-Con in July 2002. Each glass came in a red tissue-lined, heavy cardboard coffin with an embossed hand-numbered certificate as seen above. Both Series 1 and Series 2 were limited to 666 sets. Nice quality glasses with detailed etching.

Series One Barware 5 Glass Set MIB: $100-$120 ~ Single Glasses MIB: $20-$30 ea

Other Items:
Series 2 Barware
Drinking Glasses

Photos courtesy of
www.drinkwiththelivingdead.com

Series 2 barware released on April 1, 2003, like the Series 1 set, came with "Drink With The Living Dead" coasters and stickers, some assorted spiders and bugs, and the hand-numbered certificates. Each glass measures 5 3/4" tall and holds 17 oz. of your favorite liquid. Damien created the artwork used for the etching on this set. On the following pages, you will see his artwork.

Series Two Barware 5 Glass Set MIB: $100-$120 ~ Single Glasses MIB: $20-$30 ea

Other Items: Portfolios – Hand-Inked Drawings

Courtesy of Living Dead Dolls, LLC

Rare Unnumbered Portfolios & Hand Inked Drawings

Five original, unnumbered (artist proof) portfolios were offered by Damien and Ed at separate online auctions in April 2003. They were not part of the 50 original numbered pieces sold at conventions prior to the Mezco deal. Each Portfolio contained four prints that told a short story written by Ed Long and illustrated by Damien Glonek. Included in the sale of these portfolios were original 11" x 14" ink drawings of School Time Sadie, Lou Sapphire, Lizzie Borden, Deadbra Ann, and Kitty, drawn and signed by Damien Glonek, which was the original artwork etched and featured on the Series 2 Living Dead Dolls barware. The hand-inked drawings were one-of-a-kind. Also included was the "I Ate My Mommy" portfolio. Below I am listing the portfolios selling prices and the order in which they sold.

Living Dead Dolls Portfolios + Hand Inked Artwork by Damien Glonek

Deadbra Ann: $311.66 ~ Lou Sapphire: $227.50 ~ Lizzie Borden: $356.00 ~ School Time Sadie: $664.00 ~ Kitty: $778.00

Other Items:
"I Ate My Mommy" Portfolio

Photos courtesy of
www.wackystacker.com

The "I Ate My Mommy" portfolio, featuring Sadie with a short story by Ed Long and artwork by Damien Glonek, was released in 50 numbered sets. The sets came in large white envelopes and were autographed by both Damien and Ed. Portfolios like this were sold at horror conventions for $5 and were number 1 of 50, 2 of 50, etc. This artwork was later used for the design on the "I Ate My Mommy" barware set. It tells a gruesome yet funny tale about Sadie eating her mommy. The copies are on a heavy card stock and are perfect for framing. Numbered sets sell for different prices depending on the number. A lower number will bring more money then a higher number and an unnumbered set will bring slightly more than any numbered set.

I Ate My Mommy Portfolio Unnumbered Set: $100-$125

Handmade Dolls:

Prototype – Early – Rare – One–of–a Kind

I had a difficult time deciding on the best way to show off these earlier rare handmade dolls. As you can see in the first two photos, there were quite a number of different handmade dolls made and sold at horror conventions beginning in 1998. The original selling price was $40 per doll. The information and secondary market values I have compiled in the last few years, through personal sales and online auctions, has been quite extensive with selling prices ranging from $200 to $1500 per doll. Although online auctions may be a great source for finding these dolls you must understand the selling prices versus the actual values are substantially lower. Dolls selling at online auctions generally sell for one-half of the real value. Not always, but usually.

Early Handmade One of a Kind & Prototype Dolls

Some collectors have graciously allowed the use of their collections here and specified their purchase and selling prices. These dolls are rare, very hard to find, and quite expensive. Compiling this information was difficult and took over two years. The handmade dolls are continually appreciating and the estimates given here are what we might sell these dolls for in our online store *www.wackystacker.com* with premium conditions and appropriate buyers. If you would like to submit your rare dolls to our second edition, please send all submissions to email address: *LilGothicShop@wackystacker.com*.

Photos courtesy of www.wackystacker.com

Early Handmade One-of-a-Kind Sadie Doll

This rare and early Sadie doll was handmade by Damien and Ed. An avid collector of horror memorabilia who spotted the doll at the Living Dead Dolls™ booth at the Monster Bash in Pittsburgh, Pennsylvania in June 1998 purchased it for $40. Being fascinated with the look of the doll, the collector had to have it. Sadie did not come with a death certificate or coffin. She came only with a small black flower bouquet and black satin body bag. It is not clear if the body bag was original. Damien and Ed were asked to authenticate this doll and, without hesitation, they agreed this doll was handmade by them. They quickly sent an autographed Certificate of Authenticity as seen above. We sold this doll in our online store for $1,250 in October 2003. Below is an estimate of what we might sell this doll for in our online store.

Early Handmade Sadie Doll w/ Autographed Certificate of Authenticity: $1,300-$1,500

Photos courtesy of Ian Pendlebury

Early Handmade One-of-a-Kind Sin Doll

This rare and early Sin doll was handmade by Damien and Ed. It was originally purchased at the Unearthly Possessions Living Dead Dolls™ booth at a horror convention. Sin now lives in the United Kingdom with her second owner. She did not come with a death certificate. She comes with one of the original older coffins and has a small black flower bouquet. Not knowing the purchase price of this doll, I do believe the outstanding quality and originality of this doll will increase her value substantially on the secondary market. I recommend obtaining a certificate of authenticity before purchasing any of the handmade dolls. Below is an estimate of what we might sell this doll for in our online store.

Early Handmade Sin Doll w/ Coffin:
$1,300-$1,500

Photos courtesy of Ian Pendlebury

Early Handmade One-of-a-Kind Posey Doll

This rare and early Posey doll with moss in her hair was handmade by Damien and Ed and originally purchased at a Living Dead Dolls™ booth at a horror convention prior to the Mezco Toyz™ collaboration. The original selling prices for the early handmade dolls were $40 each. I've found many different one-of-a-kind Posey dolls, each with different characteristics and unique features like stakes through the hearts, flower bouquets, moss in the hair, and even sound effects. I recommend obtaining a certificate of authenticity before purchasing any of the handmade dolls. Below is an estimate of what we might sell this doll for in our online store.

Early Handmade Posey Doll w/ Moss in Hair & Coffin: $1,000-$1,200

Handmade Dolls:
Posey

Photos courtesy of Ian Pendlebury

Creep Con 2002 Handmade One-of-a-Kind Posey Doll

This Posey doll was handmade by Damien and Ed for the Creep Con Show 2002 in Baltimore, Maryland. The doll auctioned at the Living Dead Dolls™ booth and sold to the highest bidder. She is the only doll I have found to have sound effects, when you press her tummy she lets out three scary laughs. She comes with a bloody flower bouquet and autographed coffin. I recommend obtaining a certificate of authenticity before purchasing any of the handmade dolls, however, this doll does come with an autographed coffin, which in my opinion makes known her authenticity. Below is an estimate of what we might sell this doll for in our online store.

Creep Con 2002 Handmade Posey Doll w/ Sound Effects & Coffin: $1,400-$1,600

Photos courtesy of Ian Pendlebury

Early Handmade One-of-a-Kind Posey Doll

This rare and early Posey doll was handmade by Damien and Ed. She is a bloody mess with a wooden stake in her heart and original coffin and tissue paper. The handmade Posey dolls each come bare foot and have almost floor length hair. I recommend obtaining a certificate of authenticity before purchasing any of the handmade dolls. Below is an estimate of what we might sell this doll for in our online store.

Early Handmade Posey Doll w/ Stake in Heart & Coffin: $1,000-$1,100

Handmade Dolls:
Kitty

Photos courtesy of Randy and Rodonna Murawski

Handmade One-of-a-Kind Prototype Kitty Doll

Randy and Rodonna Murawski have been gracious enough to supply us with detailed information and photographs of their outstanding collection of handmade Living Dead Dolls™. They purchased many of their dolls from online auctions in 2003 and in turn sold them to collectors just one year later. This prototype doll is one of four made. One doll is missing, one was destroyed in the manufacturing process used for the Series 2 Kitty doll, and we are showing the remaining two here. The Murawskis purchased this doll in April 2003 for $1080. They took the doll to Damien and Ed and had it signed on the legs as seen above. The autographs will increase the value of the doll somewhat. Included is the original autographed coffin from where the doll was originally sold at the Chiller Theatre in October 2002. The Murawskis sold the doll to a collector in March 2004 for $1000. Below is an estimate of what we might sell this doll for in our online store.

Handmade Prototype Kitty Doll w/ Damien Glonek & Ed Long Autographs: $1,500-$1,800

Handmade Dolls:
Kitty

Photos courtesy of Jesse Soberman and Veda Darby

Handmade One-of-a-Kind Prototype Kitty Doll

Note the difference between this Kitty doll and the one on the previous page. The colors are different on the clothes, socks, chest emblem, hair ties, etc. This doll has been referred to as the orange and black Kitty. I have included a close up of the faces of both dolls so you can see why these are one-of-a-kind dolls. Note the turned up lips verses the turned down lips. This doll has a Certificate of Authenticity and coffin with a manufactured LDD sticker. Below is an estimate of what we might sell this doll for in our online store.

Handmade Prototype Kitty Doll w/ Autographed Certificate of Authenticity: $1,300-$1,500

Handmade Dolls:
Candy Rotten

Photo courtesy of Randy and Rodonna Murawski

Early Handmade One-of-a-Kind Candy Rotten Doll

This is one of five Candy Rotten dolls handmade by Ed Long in 1999. They came with different colored hair, kind of like cotton candy. I first came across this doll in April 2003 at an online auction along with a handmade Bride of Valentine. The pair of dolls was in poor condition and sold for a combined price of $515. The Murawskis then purchased Candy Rotten in June 2003 for $550 without a coffin and sold her for $800 in April 2004. All sales occurred at online auctions. This doll is very rare being the only one in existence with blue hair. Below is an estimate of what we might sell this doll for in our online store.

Early Handmade Candy Rotten Doll w/ Ed Long Autograph: $1,000-$1,200

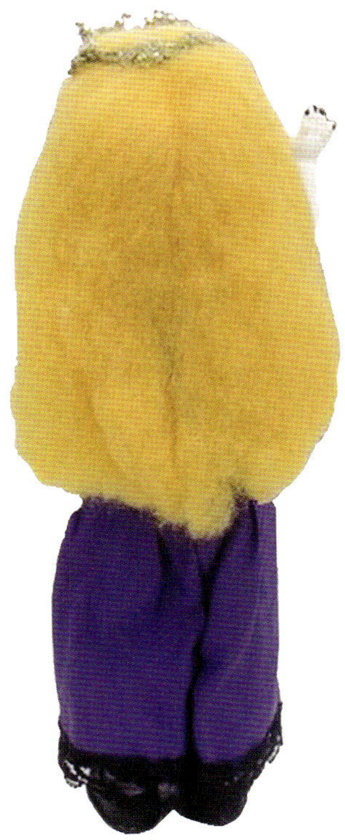

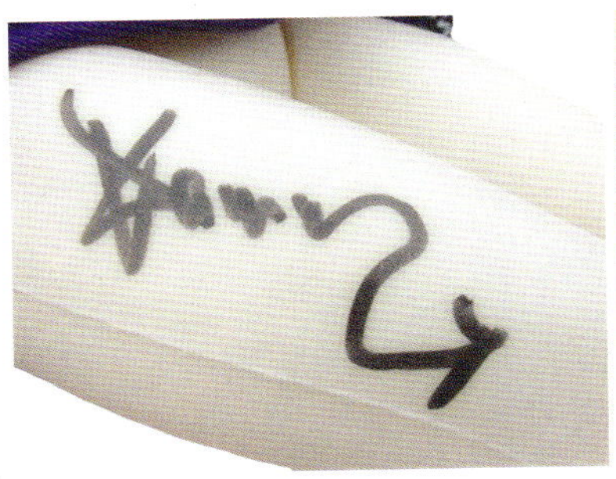

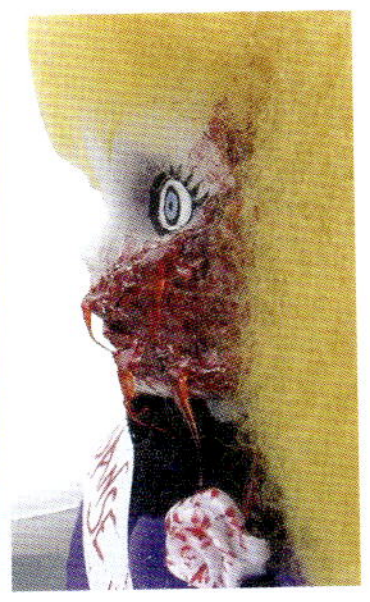

Photos courtesy of Randy and Rodonna Murawski

Handmade One-of-a-Kind Prototype Deadbra Ann Doll

There is only one of these Deadbra Ann handmade prototypes in existence. The Murkowkis purchased this doll from Damien and Ed at an online auction in May 2003 for $910. Damien, as seen above, autographed her on her right thigh. In my opinion this is by far the BEST-detailed doll they have ever made. The pictures of the open wounds on her face speak for themselves. She came with a flower bouquet and coffin. Note the skull tiara. Deadbra sold in April 2004 for $1000. Unlike some of the early handmade dolls from 1998, there is only one of these dolls in existence, which increases its value 30 to 40% or more. Below is an estimate of what we might sell this doll for in our online store.

Handmade Prototype Deadbra Ann Doll w/
Damien Glonek Autograph: $1,500-$1,800

Handmade Dolls:
Posey

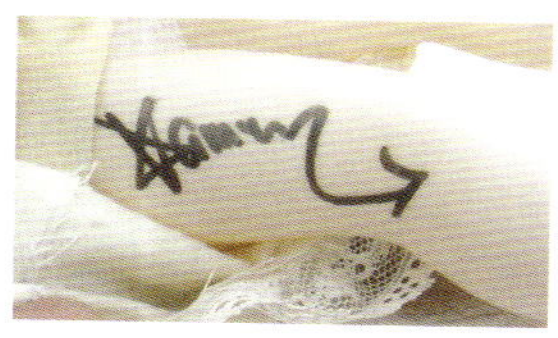

Photos courtesy of Randy and Rodonna Murawski

Early Handmade One-of-a-Kind Posey Doll

This handmade one-of-a-kind Posey from 1998 was one of the first dolls created by Damien and Ed before their partnership with Mezco Toyz™. Here is yet another variation of the Posey doll with moss in her hair and coffin. Although the Posey dolls each have unique differences, they all share the same blank stare with no pupils. Damien autographed the doll on the right thigh. The Murawskis purchased this doll in May 2003 for $700. Below is an estimate of what we would sell this doll for in our online store.

Early Handmade Posey Doll w/ Damien Glonek Autograph: $800-$1,000

Handmade Doll:
Nun – Tall Lady

Photo courtesy of A & R Computer World

Handmade One-of-a-Kind Nun Doll

This early handmade one-of-a-kind Nun doll was most likely sold at either the Chiller Theatre or Monster Bash prior to 2000. This type of doll is referred to as a "Tall Lady" and a great example of a taller 13-14" doll made by Damien and Ed. This doll is seen later in the Sinister Minister double coffin or twin-pack set as the Bad Habit. I have seen several different "Tall Lady" dolls at online auctions, with the same body styles, red eyes and either white or black hair and dresses. Below is an estimate of what we would sell this doll for in our online store.

Early Handmade Nun Tall Lady Doll w/ Handmade Coffin: $500-$600

The Holy Grail of Living Dead Dolls:

Blood-Spattered

Eggzorcist 1/30

Photo courtesy of A & R Computer World

Very Rare Blood Spattered Eggzorcist Doll 1/30

Some collectors refer to the blood-spattered Eggzorcist as the "Holy Grail" of Living Dead Dolls™. Mezco Toyz™ had thirty blood-spattered Eggzorcist dolls made as promotional items to show off their new product, Living Dead Dolls™, at the New Jersey Chiller Theatre Convention in 2000. 24 of the dolls sold at the convention for $50 each. It is not known who has the six remaining dolls. It is very difficult to track the dolls that sold as some were most likely stored, opened, or even lost. Occasionally one of these will show up at an online auction, which is where I initially found this autographed doll. It sold in March 2003 for a staggering $1825 with 13 major bids. This doll was again up for private sale in December 2003 with an asking price of $2,100. Because of the high value of this doll there are a few FAKE blood-spattered dolls circulating on the market. Use extreme caution when purchasing this doll. Below is an estimate of what we would sell this doll for in our online store.

Sealed blood spattered Eggzorcist with Damien Glonek & Ed Long Autographs: $2,000 - $2,500

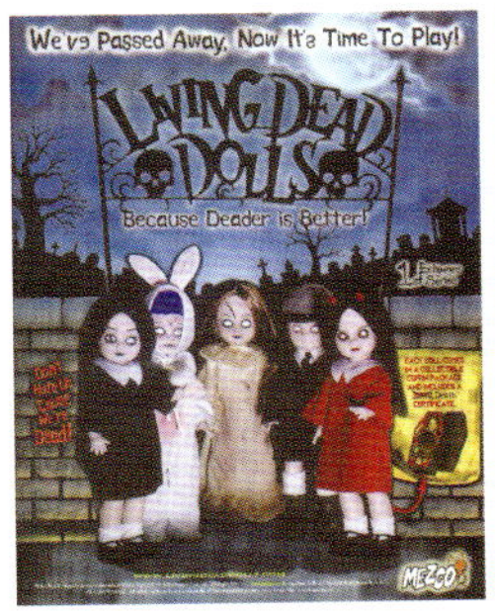

Series 1 Ad

Series 2 Ad

Series 3 Ad

I first spotted this Living Dead Dolls™ Series 1 advertisement in a Lee's Toy Review magazine back in 2000. It was not until a few years later that I actually started collecting the dolls.

Nosferatu Ad

Died & Doom Ad

Psycho-Billies Ad

These spectacular ads come out every time Mezco Toyz™ is getting ready to release a new series, exclusives, or other novelty items. I love them so much I thought they would be a great addition here.

Series 1 Fashion Victims Ad

Great Zombini Ad

American Gothic Ad

Here's a cartoon-style Fashion Victims advertisement for a new line of sexy fashion dolls. The ad read "13 of Dropped Dead Sex Appeal." I recommend collecting these colorful and creepy advertisements for a future investment. Keep your eyes peeled for them in magazines at your local bookstore.

Penny Club Mez Ad

The Dead Shall Rise Ad

This Club Mez Penny ad was run with an order form to join Club Mez in December 2001. The shadow ad "The Dead Rise Again" ran to let you know that another set of dolls was on the way, but you were not allowed to see.

Series 5th Anniversary Ad

Series 666 Ad

Series 5 was the first series to have a variation death certificate with photos from the Los Angeles Coroner's Office. Series 6 was, as some would say, a controversial ad with the number 666.

Series 666 Ad

Series 8 Ad ~ Photos courtesy of www.wackystacker.com

Series 1 Minis Ad

Series 6 ad shows the prototypes of the series used to create the set. This was the first mini series ad depicting pint-sized evil. The Series 8 ad again shows the prototypes of the series, scheduled for release in 2004.

Living Dead Dolls

SERIES I

❒ Eggzorcist $_____
❒ Sin $_____
❒ Sadie $_____
❒ Damien $_____
❒ Posey $_____

SERIES II

❒ Kitty $_____
❒ Deadbra $_____
❒ Lou $_____
❒ Schooltime Sadie $_____
❒ Lizzie $_____

SERIES III

❒Sheena $_____
❒Schitzo $_____
❒Lottie $_____
❒Lilith $_____
❒Bride $_____

SERIES IV

❒ Macumba $_____
❒ Ms Eerie $_____
❒ Inferno $_____
❒ Sybil $_____
❒ Lulu $_____

SERIES V

❒ Hollywood $_____
❒ Vincent $_____
❒ Dahlia $_____
❒ Jezebel $_____
❒ Siren $_____

SERIES V MYSTERY

❒ Hollywood $_____
❒ Vincent $_____
❒ Dahlia $_____
❒ Jezebel $_____
❒ Siren $_____

SERIES V BLOODY

❒ Hollywood $_____
❒ Vincent $_____
❒ Dahlia $_____
❒ Jezebel $_____
❒ Siren $_____

SERIES VI: 666

❒ Jinx $_____
❒ Revenant $_____
❒ Dottie w/ Eye Brows $_____
❒ Dottie w/o Eye Brows $_____
❒ Hush $_____
❒ Isaac $_____
❒ Calico $_____

SERIES VII

❒ Gluttony $_____
❒ Wrath $_____
❒ Lust $_____
❒ Envy $_____
❒ Sloth $_____
❒ Greed $_____
❒ Vanity $_____

EXCLUSIVES

❒ Died & Doom $_____
❒ Sinister Minister White $_____
❒ Sinister Minister Black $_____
❒ Sinister Minister Red $_____
#________/ 999
❒ Tragedy 1st Edit. Red $_____
❒ Tragedy 2nd Edit. Purple $_____
❒ Misery $_____
❒ Jack the Ripper UK $_____
❒ Cookie $_____
❒ Eggzorcist Bloody $_____
❒ Eggzorcist Blue Regular $_____
❒ Eggzorcist Blue Bloody $_____
❒ Psycho-Billies $_____
❒ Hazel & Hattie $_____
❒ Dr/Nurse $_____
❒ Graves & Abigail Crane $_____
❒ Series 5 Club Mez
❒ Chase Set $_____
❒ Hollywood $_____
❒ Vincent $_____
❒ Dahlia $_____
❒ Jezebel $_____
❒ Siren $_____
❒ Penny Toy2R $_____
#________/ 666
❒ Penny Club Mez $_____
❒ Bedtime Sadie Plush $_____
❒ Nosferatu & Victim $_____
❒ Walpurgis $_____
❒ Hemlock & Honey $_____
❒ Chiller Lilith Victim $_____
❒ Great Zombini & Viv $_____
❒ Jack/Jill SDCC Regular $_____
❒ Jack/Jill SDCC Bloody $_____

❐ Jack/Jill Club Mez Regular $_____
❐ Jack/Jill Club Mez Bloody $_____
❐ American Gothic $_____
❐ Captain Bonney $_____

FASHION VICTIMS I
❐ Sadie $_____
❐ Sadie Bloody $_____
❐ Lilith $_____
❐ Sheena $_____
❐ Kitty $_____

FASHION VICTIMS II
❐ Hollywood $_____
❐ Inferno $_____
❐ Sybil $_____
❐ Lulu $_____

PORCELAIN SERIES
❐ Abigail Crane $_____
❐ Posey $_____

RAGDOLLS SERIES I
❐ Moana $_____
❐ Jeepers $_____
❐ Orchid $_____
❐ Dementia Regular $_____
❐ Dementia Variant $_____

LIVING DEAD DOLLIES SERIES I
❐ Sadie $_____
❐ Lilith $_____
❐ Sheena $_____
❐ Kitty $_____
❐ Lilith Dollie Regular $_____
❐ Lilith Dollie Bloody $_____

SERIES I MINIS
❐ Eggzorcist $_____
❐ Sin $_____
❐ Sadie $_____
❐ Damien $_____
❐ Posey $_____

SERIES II MINIS
❐ Kitty $_____
❐ Deadbra $_____
❐ Lou $_____
❐ Bedtime Sadie $_____
❐ Lizzie $_____

SERIES III MINIS
❐ Sheena $_____
❐ Schitzo $_____
❐ Lottie $_____
❐ Lilith $_____
❐ Bride $_____

SERIES IV MINIS
❐ Died $_____
❐ Doom $_____
❐ Penny $_____
❐ Doctor $_____
❐ Nurse $_____

SERIES V MINIS
❐ Sybil $_____
❐ Inferno $_____
❐ Lulu $_____
❐ Macumba $_____
❐ Ms. Eerie $_____

MINI EXCLUSIVES
❐ Spencer 7pk Series I $_____
❐ Spencer 7pk Series II $_____
❐ FX Exclusive Eggzorcist $_____
❐ School time Sadie $_____
❐ Toy2R Exclusive Japan 3pk $_____
❐ Toy2R Exclusive HK 3pk $_____
❐ ClubMez Exclusive Japan 3pk $_____
❐ ClubMez Exclusive HK 3pk $_____
❐ Hot Topic Tragedy & Misery $_____

OTHER ITEMS
❐ Stationary Set Exclusive $_____
❐ Journal w/ Lock/Key $_____
❐ Pencil Sharpener Sadie $_____
❐ Pencil Sharpener Posey $_____
❐ Party Lights $_____
❐ Board Game $_____
❐ Lunch Box Tin Club Mez $_____
❐ Lunch Box Tin Series I $_____
❐ Lunch Box Tin Series II $_____
❐ Nodder Eggzorcist $_____
❐ Nodder Posey $_____
❐ Nodder Lizzie $_____
❐ Nodder Lou $_____
❐ Trading Cards Series I $_____
❐ Drinking Glasses Series I $_____
❐ Drinking Glasses Series II $_____
❐ Barware " I Ate My Mommy" $_____
❐ Pinback Button Sadie $_____
❐ Pinback Button LDD Logo $_____
❐ Sticker $_____
❐ T-Shirt $_____
❐ T-Shirt $_____
❐ T-Shirt $_____
❐ T-Shirt 5yr Tour $_____

Early Handmade Prototype Dolls

PORTFOLIOS & OTHER ITEMS

DOLL 1
Name ________________
Type ________
Size ________
Date ________
Autographed: Yes __No __
Certificate: Yes __No __
Coffin: Yes __No __
Paid $_____
Value $_____

DOLL 2
Name ________________
Type ________
Size ________
Date ________
Autographed: Yes __No __

Certificate: Yes ___No ___
Coffin: Yes ___No ___
Paid $_____
Value $_____

DOLL 3
Name ________________
Type _________
Size _________
Date _________
Autographed: Yes ___No ___
Certificate: Yes ___No ___
Coffin: Yes ___No ___
Paid $_____
Value $_____

DOLL 4
Name ________________
Type _________
Size _________
Date _________
Autographed: Yes ___No ___
Certificate: Yes ___No ___
Coffin: Yes ___No ___
Paid $_____
Value $_____

DOLL 5
Name ________________
Type _________
Size _________
Date _________
Autographed: Yes ___No ___
Certificate: Yes ___No ___
Coffin: Yes ___No ___
Paid $_____
Value $_____

DOLL 6
Name ________________
Type _________
Size _________
Date _________
Autographed: Yes ___No ___
Certificate: Yes ___No ___
Coffin: Yes ___No ___
Paid $_____
Value $_____

DOLL 7
Name ________________
Type _________
Size _________
Date _________
Autographed: Yes ___No ___
Certificate: Yes ___No ___
Coffin: Yes ___No ___
Paid $_____
Value $_____

DOLL 8
Name ________________
Type _________
Size _________
Date _________
Autographed: Yes ___No ___
Certificate: Yes ___No ___
Coffin: Yes ___No ___
Paid $_____
Value $_____

DOLL 9
Name ________________
Type _________
Size _________
Date _________
Autographed: Yes ___No ___
Certificate: Yes ___No ___
Coffin: Yes ___No ___
Paid $_____
Value $_____

DOLL 10
Name ________________
Type _________
Size _________
Date _________
Autographed: Yes ___No ___
Certificate: Yes ___No ___
Coffin: Yes ___No ___
Paid $_____
Value $_____

DOLL 11
Name ________________
Type _________
Size _________
Date _________
Autographed: Yes ___No ___
Certificate: Yes ___No ___
Coffin: Yes ___No ___
Paid $_____
Value $_____

DOLL 12
Name ________________
Type _________
Size _________
Date _________
Autographed: Yes ___No ___
Certificate: Yes ___No ___
Coffin: Yes ___No ___
Paid $_____
Value $_____

PORTFOLIO 1
Description________________
Date _________
Autographed: Yes ___No ___
__________/ 50
Info ______________
____
Paid $_____
Value $_____

PORTFOLIO 2
Description_______________
Date _________
Autographed: Yes ___No ___
___________/ 50
Info _______________
____
Paid $_____
Value $_____

PORTFOLIO 3
Description_______________
Date _________
Autographed: Yes ___No ___
___________/ 50
Info _______________
____
Paid $_____
Value $_____

PORTFOLIO 4
Description_______________
____
Date _________
Autographed: Yes ___No ___
___________/ 50
Info _______________
____
Paid $_____
Value $_____

PORTFOLIO 5
Description_______________
____
Date _________
Autographed: Yes ___No ___
___________/ 50
Info _______________
____
Paid $_____
Value $_____

PORTFOLIO 6
Description_______________
____
Date _________
Autographed: Yes ___No ___
___________/ 50
Info _______________
____
Paid $_____
Value $_____

OTHER ITEM 1
Description_______________
____
Date _________
Autographed: Yes ___No ___
Certificate: Yes ___No ___
Info _______________
____
Paid $_____
Value $_____

OTHER ITEM 2
Description_______________
____
Date _________
Autographed: Yes ___No ___
Certificate: Yes ___No ___
Info _______________
____
Paid $_____
Value $_____

OTHER ITEM 3
Description_______________
____
Date _________
Autographed: Yes ___No ___
Certificate: Yes ___No ___
Info _______________
____
Paid $_____
Value $_____

OTHER ITEM 4
Description_______________
____
Date _________
Autographed: Yes ___No ___
Certificate: Yes ___No ___
Info _______________
____
Paid $_____
Value $_____

OTHER ITEM 5
Description_______________
____
Date _________
Autographed: Yes ___No ___
Certificate: Yes ___No ___
Info _______________
____
Paid $_____
Value $_____

OTHER ITEM 6
Description_______________
____
Date _________
Autographed: Yes ___No ___
Certificate: Yes ___No ___
Info _______________
____
Paid $_____
Value $_____

OTHER ITEM 7
Description_______________
____
Date _________
Autographed: Yes ___No ___
Certificate: Yes ___No ___
Info _______________
____
Paid $_____
Value $_____

OTHER ITEM 8
Description_______________
____
Date _________
Autographed: Yes ___No ___
Certificate: Yes ___No ___
Info _______________
____
Paid $_____
Value $_____

OTHER ITEM 9
Description_______________
____
Date _________
Autographed: Yes ___No ___
Certificate: Yes ___No ___
Info _______________
____
Paid $_____
Value $_____

OTHER ITEM 10
Description_______________
____
Date _________
Autographed: Yes ___No ___
Certificate: Yes ___No ___
Info _______________
____
Paid $_____
Value $_____

OTHER ITEM 11
Description_______________
____
Date _________
Autographed: Yes ___No ___
Certificate: Yes ___No ___
Info _______________
____
Paid $_____
Value $_____

OTHER ITEM 12
Description_______________
____
Date _________
Autographed: Yes ___No ___
Certificate: Yes ___No ___
Info _______________
____
Paid $_____
Value $_____

Bleeding Edge™ Goths:

Series 1 Fashion Dolls

Storm

Lillian

Raven

Sinstress

Raven

Photos courtesy of www.wackystacker.com

Malice

Bleeding Edge™ Goths entered the scene in July 2002 with a set a five 12" gothic fashion dolls and four 7" vinyl figurines, creations of Steve Varner. Although the dolls do not include accessories, they have a unique style, which includes exotic clothing, metal piercing, and hairstyles. More like fashion plates from a scene in a New York nightclub from the 1940s, the dolls are pale-skinned gothic fashion beauties without blood and gore. The dolls feature bendable plastic and rubber bodies. Prices given below are for dolls, which are mint in box.

Storm: $30-$35 ~ Lillian: $20-$25 ~ Raven: $25-$30 ~ Sintress: $20-$25 ~ Malice: $20-$25

Bleeding Edge™ Goths:
Series 1 Chase & Variation Dolls

Liliian black jacket & belt variation

Lillian black jacket & red belt variation

Malice red bangs variation

Photos courtesy of www.wackystacker.com

Several limited chase and variation dolls exist with each series. The original Lillian doll came with a red-lined jacket and a red belt. A second Lillian was made that included an all-black jacket and belt. When the manufacturer ran out of black belts for the second version of Lillian, they simply used the red belts left over from the first version and therefore we have three different Lillian dolls. Production numbers are unknown. I would assume the latter would be the rarest of all. Malice with red bangs is limited to 1,200 pieces. Prices given below are for dolls, which are mint in box.

Lillian all black: \$50-\$70 ~ Lillian black w/ red belt: \$80-\$100 ~ Malice red bangs: \$50-\$70

Bleeding Edge™ Goths: Series 2 Fashion Dolls

Casual Storm

Abcynthia Chaser

Angelina Blasphemina

Suzisin Ful

Angelina Blasphemina

Victoria Creeper

Photos courtesy of www.wackystacker.com

Series 2 is yet another great line up with five dolls and the same great quality and designs. Suzisin Ful even comes with a pair of wooden chopsticks in her hair. I recommend adding Bleeding Edge™ Goths to your collection of gothic dolls before the prices go any higher and they will. With a worldwide fan base values are steadily climbing. Prices given below are for dolls, which are mint in box.

Casual Storm: $20-$25 ~ Abcynthia: $25-$30 ~ Angelina: $20-$25 ~ Suzisin: $20-$25 ~ Victoria: $20-$25

Bleeding Edge™ Goths:
Series 2 Chase & Variation Dolls

Suzisin Ful black & red hair variation

Angelina Blasphemina blue hair variation

Victoria Creep pink hair variation

Photos courtesy of www.wackystacker.com

Series 2 includes three chase or variation dolls, which are Suzisin Ful with black & red hair instead of white & black hair. Angelina Blasphemina has blue hair and black streaks instead of black hair with blue streaks. Victoria Creeper has hot pink hair and a black jacket instead of white hair and a burgundy jacket. The values of the chase or variation dolls are slightly higher then the regular dolls. Most of them are limited to 1,200 pieces or less.

Suzisin Ful Chase MIB: $40-$50 ~ Angelina Blasphemina Chase MIB: $40-$50 ~ Victoria Creeper Chase MIB: $40-$50

Bleeding Edge™ Goths:
Series 3 Fashion Dolls

Divinity

Julia Doom

Serpentina Maria Sangria

Back to School Storm

Photos courtesy of Bleeding Edge™ Goths

Scorpio Vixen

Series three was released in October 2004 as a five dolls set. Each series has contained a variation of the Storm doll, which has proven to be the most popular doll manufactured to date. Chase and variations dolls do exist although we have not shown them here. Prices given below are for dolls, which are mint in box.

Divinity: \$20-\$25 ~ Julia: \$20-\$25 ~ Serpentina: \$20-\$25 ~ Back to School Storm: \$20-\$25 ~ Scorpio: \$25-\$30

Bleeding Edge™ Goths: Exclusives

Lolita Sun

Siphon Veins ~ Photos courtesy of Bleeding Edge™ Goths

Lolita Sun was released as a figures.com exclusive limited to 3,000 pieces in April 2003 and originally sold for $29.99. She was the first exclusive produced. Siphon Veins, made exclusively for the San Diego Comic Con in July 2004 and was limited to 1,000 pieces only. Siphon featured a new body style created by the company with a snarling lip and fangs. There are several exclusives not pictured here that are available through the Bleeding Edge™ online Crypt Club.

Lolita Sun MIB: $40-$50 ~ Siphon Veins MIB: $50-$60

Bleeding Edge™ Goths: Series 1 Vinyl Figurines

Belladonna

Morbida

Dagger

Wormwood

Morbida SDCC Exclusive

Wormwood black vest variation ~ Photos courtesy of Bleeding Edge™ Goths and www.wackystacker.com

Bleeding Edge™ Goths released the Series 1, 7" vinyl figurines on the heels of their Series 1, 12" fashion dolls. Unlike the dolls, the figurines have some different points of articulation at the waist, arms, biceps, and necks. The figurines have amazing detail and even feature intricate tattoos and metal piercing. Prices given below are for figurines mint in the box. The black vest Wormwood variation is limited to 2,500 pieces and the SDCC Morbida is limited to 2,000 pieces.

Belladonna: $10-$12 ~ Morbida: $20-$25 ~ Dagger: $10-12 ~ Wormwood/Red Vest: $10-$14 ~ Morbida SDCC Exclusive: $30-$40 ~ Wormwood/Black Vest: $16-$20

Bleeding Edge™ Goths: Series 2 Vinyl Figurines

Hysteria Venom

Ophelia Pain

Trinity Tortura

Hysteria Venom brown variation

Dru Id bizarre make-up variation

Dru Id ~ Photos courtesy of Bleeding Edge™ Goths and www.wackystacker.com

As with the 12" fashion dolls, each series of figurines includes some chase or variation pieces. Included in Series 2 are a tan or brown skinned Hysteria Venom and a Dru Id with bizarre make-up, both limited to 2,500 pieces only. The Hysteria variation is extremely limited in the United States and difficult to find. Prices given below are for figurines, which are mint in box.

Hysteria Venom: $12-$14 ~ Ophelia Pain: $13-$15 ~ Trinity Totura: $13-15 ~ Hysteria brown variation: $40-$50 ~ Dru Id bizarre make-up variation: $15-$20 ~ Dru Id: $12-$14

Bleeding Edge™ Goths: Series 3 Vinyl Figurines

Autumn von Sanguine

Eva Destruction

Veronika Despair

Nurse Hypochondrianna

Photos courtesy of Bleeding Edge™ Goths

Series 3 figurines were released as a set of 4 in October 2004. The series included some chase or variation pieces not pictured here. Look for more great fashion dolls and figurines coming soon from Bleeding Edge™ Goths.

Autumn MIB: $14-$15 ~ Eva MIB: $14-$15 ~ Veronika MIB: $14-$15 ~ Nurse Hypo MIB: $14-$15

Krypt Kiddies™

Vintage doll repairer and collector Rita Uhl and her husband, horror artist Ed Uhl, created Krypt Kiddies™ in May 2002. Rita started out making dolls called "reborns" using a technique that makes the dolls look and feel real. Ed added his creepy horror artist twist and thus Krypt Kiddies™ were born.

The Uhls started out selling their handmade dolls via their website, at conventions and online auctions. Collectors quickly accepted their creepy creations with great enthusiasm. They soon met with Spencer Gifts in January 2003, where they agreed to a partnership to mass-produce a line of their dolls and to include six pairs each year, see following page.

The handmade dolls can still be special ordered from Rita and Ed at their online store, www.kryptkiddies.com, with prices starting from $120 each. The handmade dolls measure 17" tall, come with custom certificates and may include accessories upon request. The Uhls are just getting started so you can be sure to see some more creepy Krypt Kiddies™.

Abigorey 2003

Albina 2002

Drusilla 2002 ~ Photos courtesy of Rita & Ed Uhl

Singe and Scorch 2004

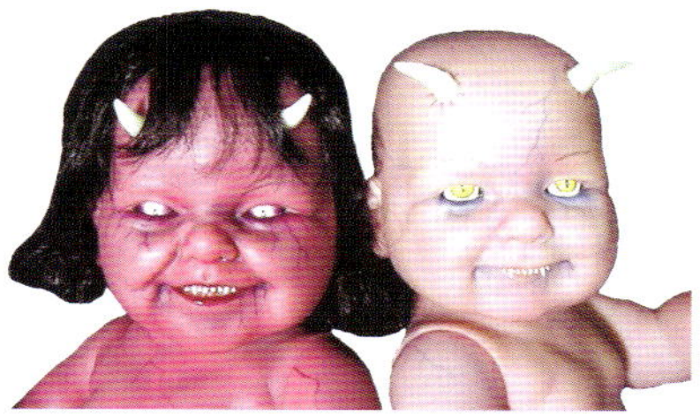

Vile-ette and Wretched 2004

Azure and Sourpuss 2004

Kim and Horrous 2004

Krypt Kiddies™

Devilynne and Demion

Devilynne and Demion, the first set of Krypt Kiddies™, released as a Spencer Gifts exclusive on May 12, 2004 for $29.99 each. Separately packaged the dolls come with a blood baby bottle, certificate and measure approx. 15″ tall.

Ivory and Bill Z Bob

Ivory and Bill Z Bob, the second of three sets in the series scheduled for release July 27, 2004. The Uhls have stated they have made around 300 one-of-a-kind handmade dolls with values ranging from $150 and up and hope to bring collectors many more creations through their collaboration with Spencer Gifts.

Raven and Azeal

Photos courtesy of Frank Mitman Photographer

Raven and Azeal, the final set in the series scheduled for release November 1, 2004. Manufactured Krypt Kiddies™ sold exclusively at Spencer Gifts; however, you will be sure to find these on the secondary market in the very near future.

Teddy Scares™

Teddy Scares™ are an awesome new twist on the teddy bear created by childhood friends Phil Nannay and Joe DiDomenico. I met Phil and Joe at the Comic-Con Las Vegas where the scary bears made their debut in October 2003. I love the Teddy Scares™ so much I thought they would be a nice addition here. In fact I asked Phil and Joe for some pictures and they sent me this way wicked cool press kit packed in a real wooden crate with creepy stickers saying the contents may cause insanity and crammed full of cool stuff.

Five 12" plush bears were released with real cloth clothing, killer accessories, and even a toe tag. Teddy Scares™ come packaged in a window display box; you can't keep your eyes off of it. There is so much happening on the box before you even get to the bears. Each bear has a unique obituary that includes a death date and a creepy poem. The bears are getting harder to find with Edwin Morose and Hester Golem being the most popular among collectors. I recommend starting this collection soon if you haven't done so already.

Abnormal Cyrus MIB: $25-$30 ~ Edwin Morose MIB: $30-$35 ~ Redmond Gore MIB: $25-$30

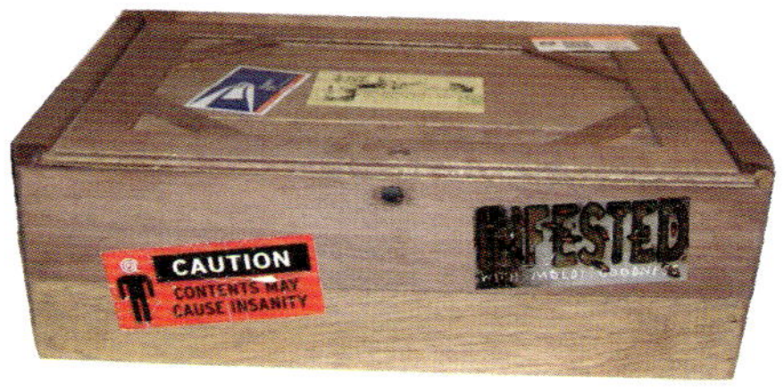

Sealed press kit mailer

Opened press kit mailer ~ Photos courtesy of www.wackystacker.com

Abnormal Cyrus

Edwin Morose

Redmond Gore ~ Photos courtesy of the Applehead Factory Inc.

Teddy Scares™

Hester Golem

Photos courtesy of the Applehead Factory Inc.

Edwin Morose club exclusive

Hester Golem is one of the most sought-after of the Teddy Scares™ bears, being limited to 3,334 pieces only. He is extremely hard to find and you can expect to pay a minimum of $50 for this bear if you can find him. A variation of the Edwin Morose bear was recently released and made his debut at the San Diego Comic Con in July 2004. The bear is also available at their Teddy Scares™ "Barely Alive Online Club."

Rita Mortis autographed red eye dye variation

Rita Mortis black dye eye variation

Photos courtesy of the Applehead Factory Inc. and www.wackystacker.com

Rita Mortis was originally produced with red dye around red button eyes. The company did not like the way the bear looked and had her changed to black dye instead. There were 1,100 pieces manufactured with red dye that makes this one of the rarest and hard to find bears, though it is not very well known among collectors. The estimated production run for the remaining bears is said to be right around 5,000 to 6,000 pieces.

Hester Golem MIB: $50-$75 ~ Rita Mortis Black Dye MIB: $30-$35 ~ Autographed Rita Red Dye MIB: $100-$150